Child Abuse

Recognition and Management

Child Abuse

Recognition and Management

Debbie Warley RGN, Diploma in Professional Practice,
ENB 199, ENB 998

*Senior Staff Nurse, Accident & Emergency,
Maidstone General Hospital, Maidstone, UK*

and

Julie Pettet RGN, Diploma in Professional Practice,
ENB 199, ENB 998

*Senior Staff Nurse, Accident & Emergency,
Maidstone General Hospital, Maidstone, UK*

SCUTARI PRESS ● LONDON

Scutari Press   24–28 Oval Road
London NW1 7DX, UK

The Curtis Center
Independence Square West
Philadelphia, PA 19106–3399, USA

Harcourt Brace & Company
55 Horner Avenue
Toronto, Ontario M8Z 4X6, Canada

Harcourt Brace & Company, Australia
30–52 Smidmore Street
Marrickville, NSW 2204, Australia

Harcourt Brace & Company, Japan
Ichibancho Central Building, 22–1 Ichibancho
Chiyoda-ku, Tokyo 102, Japan

© 1997 Scutari Press

This book is printed on acid-free paper

A catalogue record for this book is available from the British Library

ISBN 1-873852-44-4

Typeset by Phoenix Photosetting, Chatham, Kent
Printed in Great Britain by St Edmundsbury Press Ltd,
Bury St Edmunds, Suffolk

Contents

Introduction   1

1. Recognition of Abuse   3
2. Assessment Guidelines   7
3. Physical Abuse   11
4. Sexual Abuse   25
5. Emotional Abuse   43
6. Munchausen's Syndrome by Proxy   55
7. Fatal Abuse   61
8. Management of Child Abuse   65
9. Accountability   81

References   83

Bibliography   87

Introduction

The existence of child abuse has been recognised for a very long time. What is new is the willingness to recognise its existence and to look for ways of preventing its occurrence. There is evidence that 100 years ago child abuse was culturally acceptable in Britain:

> The evils are enormous and indisputable, but they are so private, internal and domestic a character as to be beyond the reach of legislation and the subject would not, I think, be entertained in either house of Parliament.
> **Lord Shaftesbury, 1880**

It is ironic that the first charter for children was introduced in 1889, some 67 years after the legislation to protect animals.

The true incidence of child abuse in the UK is unknown, although as Lloyd de Mause (1980) reports, 'since the 18th century a more humanitarian attitude has gradually emerged'.

However, the change in attitudes is slow and faltering. In 1895, the NSPCC reported that children were battered with 'boots, crockery, pans, shovels, straps, ropes, pokers, fire and boiling water'. Almost a century later, Newson and Newson (1986) found that by the age of seven, 26 per cent of boys and 18 per cent of girls had been hit with an implement, and a further 53 per cent (65 per cent boys and 41 per cent girls) threatened.

It is not possible to provide a single comprehensive theory by which to understand child abuse. History gives us perspective which helps us understand our shortcomings towards children. The danger is that we should pretend that the lives of children now are very different.

> If in people's minds child abuse remains unthinkable, then progress cannot be made.
> **(Hobbs et al, 1993)**

It is for this reason that we decided to compile this book to serve as an education pack for staff on the recognition and management of child abuse. Through increased public awareness, better professional recognition and an unwillingness by society to tolerate the abuse of children, we should see a decrease in the incidence of child abuse. However, until this happens:

- Every day in Britain 75 children will be added to child protection registers.

Department of Health, 1992

- Child abuse will remain the fourth commonest cause of death in pre-school children.

Browne et al., 1991

- This week at least four children in Britain will die as a result of abuse or neglect.

Meadow, 1993

1

Recognition of Abuse

It shouldn't hurt to be a child

Child abuse is common – frighteningly so. Some acts of cruelty are unthinkable and therefore we are tempted to ignore its existence. But we have to remember children are dependent on adults to survive. They are dependent on society for standards of behaviour and if we close our eyes to the horrors of this cruelty then we are just as responsible as those who abuse children.

The effects of child abuse are devastating and wide reaching. They affect the way the child grows into an adult and have 'ripple effects' on their subsequent relationships and families. Their perception of society's values and morals are distorted so there is the possibility of abuse to their children.

As healthcare professionals we are responsible for any child that comes into our care. But as individuals in society we are also responsible for acknowledging the existence of child abuse. By knowing the signs, symptoms and effects of abuse we can be more aware and act on any suspicions that are raised. Also, by passing on knowledge we can go a long way to reducing the incidence of cruelty to children and therefore improve the outlook for their future.

The following chapters cover different aspects of abuse from recognition through to management. It can be used as a guide or a reference for professionals that come into contact with children. For every professional who is made aware of the signs, symptoms and effects of child abuse this may be one child that is saved.

PRESENTATION

Direct report

This may be made by a child, a parent or other interested third party. Most reports like this are genuine and should be believed. Worries by grandparents and other responsible family members need careful assessment. The reasons for the reports need to be identified even if no obvious abuse is found.

Presentation of an injury

Things to look out for which may indicate physical abuse include:

- Repetitive pattern of injury, but parents may visit different hospitals to avoid detection.

- Injuries not consistent with the history, for example, too many, too severe, wrong kind, wrong distribution, wrong age.

- Patterns of injury which strongly suggest abuse include:
  Bruising to a young baby.
  Multiple injuries following a moderate fall.
  Severe head injuries in babies or toddlers.
  Rib fractures.
  Subdural haematoma and retinal haemorrhage from violent shaking.
  Multiple cigarette burns.
  Fractures in infants and toddlers particularly under 3 years of age.
  The presence of other signs of abuse, for example, neglect, failure to thrive or sexual abuse.

- Unusual behaviour in the parents:
  Delay in seeking advice.
  Refusal to allow proper treatment or admission to hospital.
  Unprovoked aggression towards staff.

Hobbs et al. 1993

Incidental discovery of an injury

Abused children are frequently allowed to go to school or nursery or another person's care where the abuse may be discovered. It is not unusual for parents to deny all knowledge and to give no satisfactory explanation.

FEATURES IN THE HISTORY

Discrepant history

Does the story change with telling? Who tells the story? Is it vague or unclear? Do the mother and father tell the same story? Are they able to give exact details of the accident?

Unreasonable delay

This is a strong indicator of abuse when there is delay in seeking help following an accident to a child, particularly with a burn or fracture. It is common to deny that the child was in pain and to minimise the injury (Hobbs et al, 1993).

Family crisis

A complicated home situation or family crisis may have precipitated the injury, for example, bereavement, loss of a job or break-up of a relationship. In these circumstances the parents are usually willing to reveal what happened if someone is prepared to listen to them.

Trigger factors

There may be behaviours in the child which precipitate the parents' violence, for example inconsolable crying at night, bed-wetting, or in the older child, lying or stealing.

Parental history of abuse

Many research articles have shown that parents who abuse their children were abused themselves as children (Egeland, 1991). Some may also have been in care.

Unrealistic expectations

This is linked to a poor understanding of child development. The child is expected to love his parents. When he cries or refuses his feeds, parents may see this as rejection or punishment.

Social isolation

This is common in parents who abuse (Hobbs et al, 1993). Parents may feel isolated from friends, extended family and professionals. As the abuse escalates, parents find it increasingly difficult to allow anyone into their lives for fear of discovery.

Past history of the child

The presence of high levels of parental anxiety, frequent attendances at hospital in the first few months of life and so-called 'accident-prone' children may be a sign that parents are having difficulties coping. They may be overly anxious about the child's weight, growth, health or behaviour. These anxieties may be minimised in their desire to present themselves as perfect parents.

2

Assessment Guidelines

It is important to check the Accident and Emergency (A&E) card at the beginning of any paediatric assessment to ensure all details are complete. If it becomes necessary to make a social services/health visitor referral later, this will be easier if as much information as possible is available about the child. This information should be checked for all paediatric attendances, not just suspected non-accidental injury. All paediatric A&E cards should contain the following information:

- name, address and telephone number;
- age and date of birth;
- name and address of general practitioner;
- school/nursery the child attends; .
- name of health visitor;
- next of kin: parent/guardian.

KEY POINTS

Abuse and neglect is a major cause of injury in children.

1. An estimated 10 per cent of all injuries sustained by children seen in accident and emergency departments are a result of child abuse (Scherb, 1988).

2. Head and abdominal injuries constitute the majority of severe injuries and deaths (Hobbs, 1991).

3. Abuse is rarely an isolated event – it recurs and is progressive (Scherb, 1988).

4. A&E nurses must develop a high index of suspicion while treating children with injuries.

5. Staff in the A&E department are the most frequent reporters of child abuse (Scherb, 1988).

ASSESSMENT

1. Age and past medical history, including pregnancy, infections and recurrent injuries.

2. History from care giver:

- Identify relationship between care giver and child.

- Note any changes in the child's behaviour.

- Consider the explanation for the injury or presenting condition; does the parent or carer:

  a) fail or show reluctance to explain injury or condition;

  b) give an unsatisfactory, inconsistent or conflicting history of injury or condition;

  c) give history of 'problem child';

  d) give history of accident-proneness;

  e) give history of unwanted or unplanned pregnancy;

  f) give history of abuse or neglect as a child.

(Scherb, 1988)

3. History from child:

- reports incident(s) of abuse or neglect;

- gives different story of injury or condition than care giver.

4. Mechanism of injury:

- Explanation is inconsistent with the developmental ability of the child.

- Explanation is inconsistent with the type and severity of injury.

(Jurgrau, 1990)

5. Vital signs, height and weight – compare with figures on centile chart.

6. Attitude and behaviour of care giver:

- appears overly concerned or shows lack of concern;

- displays defensive behaviour or anger;

- reacts inappropriately to child's injury, for example by crying;

- is reluctant to allow other tests to be carried out which may reveal earlier injuries;

- be aware of the care giver who refuses to remain at the hospital, even if the child is admitted;

- is there evidence of drug or alcohol abuse in the care giver?

(Leatherland, 1986)

7. Behaviour of the child:

- shows inappropriate response to people or pain – a child who shows no apprehension may be a victim of abuse who is accustomed to living with fear (Jurgrau, 1990);

- shows developmental abilities inappropriate for age;

- displays inappropriate sexual behaviour or mannerisms;

- shows reluctance to undress or to be examined (recognise age and cultural differences);

- child wears unseasonal clothing to cover injuries.

8. Physical assessment of the child:

- overall appearance, cleanliness, nourishment and health of the child.

3

Physical Abuse

DEFINITION

> Physical abuse to a child, including deliberate poisoning, where there is definite knowledge, or reasonable suspicion, that the injury was inflicted or knowingly not prevented.
> **Department of Health, 1992**

Hobbs et al (1993) further include suffocation and Munchausen's syndrome by proxy.

Within this definition, hitting a child does not constitute physical abuse unless it results in injury.

FACTS AND FIGURES

Official reporting represents only a fraction of the total number of cases in the population as a whole.

Reporting depends on awareness of the problem by the public and professionals including doctors, nurses, social workers, teachers and others in contact with children.

Such awareness tends to increase following the reporting of a particularly serious, often fatal, case by the media. Referrals then tend to rise for a while.

Department of Health (1992) figures show that in March 1991:

- there was a total of 45 300 children on the child protection registers in England;

- of these, 28 000 were new registrations since March 1990.

Creighton and Noyes (1990) estimate that:

- 200–230 non-accidental deaths occur each year in Britain.

- 1.5–2 per cent of all children will have been physically abused by the age of 17.

- Boys outnumber girls: in 1987, 55 per cent were boys, 45 per cent girls.

- Nearly half of the children are aged 0–4 years.

Hobbs and Wynne (1990) report that physical abuse rarely exists on its own. It is important to recognise its links with other forms of abuse:

- 1 in 6 physically abused children have also been sexually abused. Others have been neglected or have failed to thrive.

- Emotional abuse exists in most cases.

- Physical abuse occurs in children of all ethnic groups.

Handicapped children are at increased risk. Smith and Hanson (1974) reported that 13.5 per cent of physically abused children had handicaps.

SOCIAL BACKGROUND

- Physical abuse occurs more commonly in conditions of social deprivation and poverty.

- 67 per cent of mothers and 52 per cent of fathers are unemployed.

- Families tend to be larger, for example, four or more children.

- Nearly half of the children abused are first born.

- Natural parents or parent figures were responsible for the abuse in 90 per cent of cases.   (Creighton and Noyes, 1989)

BRUISES

Bruises are present in 90 per cent of physically abused children (Hobbs et al, 1993). Multiple bruises have often been inflicted on a number of occasions and are of different age, size and shape. After a single accident, bruises will be of the same age and few in number.

It is important to be able to give a rough estimate of the age of individual bruises. Table 3.1 provides a guide to determining the age of bruises.

Age	Colour
less than 24 hours	red/purple
12–24 hours	purplish/blue
48–72 hours	brown
older than 72 hours	yellow

Table 3.1. Approximate age of bruises by appearance (Speight, 1993)

General points

- Bruises on the buttocks, lower back and outer thighs are often related to punishment.

- Bruises to the inner thighs and genital area suggest child sexual abuse or punishment for toileting misdemeanours.

- The penis may be pulled or pinched and sometimes tied with string.

- Slap marks are found on the sides of the face or ears.

- Bruises to the ears are rarely accidental. They fall within the 'triangle of safety' – the protective effect of the triangle created by the shoulder, skull and base of the neck greatly reduces injury to the ear following a fall.

- Bruises to the lower jaw and mastoid are strongly indicative of abuse.

- Bruises around the neck, eyes and mouth suggest choking and may present as a petechial rash.

- A black eye in older children can be as a result of a direct blow, but it takes extreme force to cause bilateral black eyes.

- Injuries to the upper lip and frenulum may indicate forced feeding.

- Bruises distal to the elbow and knees are generally less significant than those on the upper arms and thighs.

- Bruises to the chest and abdomen are suspicious of abuse and lower abdominal bruises should suggest child sexual abuse.

(Hobbs et al 1993).

Patterns of bruises

Inflicted bruises show a number of different patterns:

Hand marks
- Grab marks or fingertip bruises, e.g. on limbs or chest wall.

- Hand prints or linear finger marks.

- Slap marks – two or three finger-sized linear marks can be seen with a stripe effect. Rings leave a tell-tale mark.

- Pinch marks – a pair of crescent-shaped bruises facing one another.

- Poking marks – fingernail may cut the skin.

Marks from implements
- Belts or straps leave curves with the contours of the body, whereas stick marks are less clearly defined and are usually thinner.

- Newson and Newson (1986) found that in a sample of 700 children, 26 per cent of boys and 18 per cent of girls had been hit with an implement by the age of 7.

- Loops of flex show circular closed thin lines.

- Ties or ligatures cause circumferential bands around limbs and gags cause abrasions at the corner of the mouth.

Bite marks

- Bites can be animal or human, and made by an adult or a child.

- Identification of the perpetrator is only possible if the mark is recent and clear.

Bizarre marks

- Unusual bruises may arise when a child is struck through clothes when the pattern of the weave may be apparent.

Kicks

- These usually occur on the lower half of the body. They cause large, irregularly shaped bruises occasionally reflecting the shape of the shoe (Hobbs et al., 1993).

FRACTURES

Fractures caused by abuse usually result from the more extreme forms of violence and represent serious injury. They may coexist with other signs of trauma, for example bruises, scratches, subdural haematoma, retinal haemorrhage or ruptured gut. Fractures may occur in any bone, being single or multiple, clinically obvious or occult and only detected by radiography.

It was the recognition of fractures that prompted Caffey (1946) to identify the parent–infant stress syndrome, later renamed the battered baby syndrome (Kempe et al 1962). Since that time, the connection of injury to the child has widened. Injury to almost every bone has been described as abuse, but certain patterns have emerged and our understanding of the relationship between causes and effect has improved.

Fractures – abuse or accident?

In the first year of life, fractures are more likely to be as a result of abuse than at any other time (Hobbs, 1993a). A high index of suspicion is therefore required.

Herndon (1983) studied physically abused children and found that 58 per cent were under 3 years of age and sustained 95 per cent of the fractures.

In non-abused children Worlock et al (1986) found that 85 per cent of fractures occur over the age of 5. Therefore the majority of fractures resulting from abuse occur in infants and pre-school children. The significance of bone fractures is summarised in Table 3.2.

Bone	Fracture type	Abuse	Accident
Humerus	spiral/oblique	++	+
	supracondylar	+	+
	metaphysis	+++	+−
Forearm	shaft	direct/indirect injury	common
	metaphysis	uncommon	rare
Hand	shaft	occasionally described	uncommon
Femur	shaft	under 2 yrs high risk	older child
	metaphysis	+++(lower end)	uncommon
Tibia	shaft-periosteal	+	−
	spiral	+	+
	metaphysis	++	rare
Fibula	shaft	kick +	+
	metaphysis	+	rare
Foot	metaphysis	highly specific uncommon pre-school	−
Pelvis	pubic ramus	periosteal reaction	only after major trauma
Scapula	various injuries	indirect force, high specificity	rare

+, possibility of abuse; +++, high risk of abuse, injury unlikely to be due to accident; −, less frequently seen in injuries due to abuse.

Table 3.2. Significance of bone fractures (Hobbs et al 1993)

Points to remember

- Fractures are sudden, painful and lead to immediate loss of function.

- If a child does not cry or express pain, ask why. Abused children are sometimes too frightened to complain; the frozen watchful child can be recognised in the A&E department.

- Children do not continue to walk or play with a fracture, but parents who have abused may ignore the injury.

- Pain is maximum at the beginning. As the bruising and swelling develops, the pain may lessen.

- Many fractures show no bruising.

Patterns of injury in abuse

- A single fracture with multiple bruises.

- Multiple fractures in different stages of healing, possibly with no bruises or soft tissue injuries.

- Metaphyseal-epiphyseal injuries which are often multiple.

- Rib fractures.

- The formation of new periosteal bone.

- A skull fracture in association with intracranial injury.

Rib fractures

Usually occult and detected only by radiography. In infants the ribs are very pliable and unless there is bone disease, severe trauma can be assumed. Cardiopulmonary trauma is not responsible (Feldman and Brewer, 1984). The fractures are often multiple, bilateral and posterior and are thought to follow thoracic compression during shaking episodes or kicking.

Metaphyseal and epiphyseal fractures

These are classic injuries of physical abuse. A fragment of bone becomes separated from the end of a long bone either as a chip or as a whole plate. Such injuries arise from acceleration and deceleration as the infant is shaken by the body, arms or legs. The usual sites are the knee, wrist, elbow and ankle.

Fractures of the shafts of long bones

Abuse injuries commonly arise when a limb is grasped, twisted, pulled or used as a handle to swing or shake the child. Certain fractures are more common in abuse, for example, spiral humeral, femoral in infancy (up to 80 per cent abuse), lateral clavicular, and small bones of hands and feet (Hobbs et al, 1993).

- Transverse fractures are the result of angulation following a direct blow.

- Oblique transverse fractures are the result of angulation.

- Spiral fractures are the result of twisting.

- Oblique fractures are the result of angulation.

Skeletal survey

A skeletal survey should be considered in the following situations:

- Presentation with a fracture which suggests abuse.

- Physically abused children under 3 years of age.

- Older children with severe soft tissue injury.

- Localised pain, limp or reluctance to use a limb.

- Previous history of recent skeletal injury.

- Unexplained neurological signs or symptoms.

- Child dying in suspicious or unusual circumstances.

Hobbs et al (1993)

HEAD INJURIES

Head injury is the major cause of death following physical abuse (Hobbs, 1993b). The head is the commonest target for assault in the young child. In the first year of life, 95 per cent of serious intracranial injury is the result of abuse.

There are two categories of head injury:

- Focal from impacts – punches, hitting the head due to throwing or swinging the child on or against an object or surface.

- Diffuse injury from acceleration – shaking.

A combination of the two is thought to account for many serious injuries.

Between 40 and 70 per cent of abused children have some form of injury to the face or head. These include bruises to the face or scalp, traumatic alopecia and subgaleal haematoma, skull or facial fracture, subdural or subarachnoid haemorrhage, cerebral contusion and oedema.

Skull fractures

The most commonly fractured bone, either in abuse or accident, is the parietal bone which is large, thin, prominent and vulnerable to injury. Frontal fractures are much less commonly seen, either in abuse or following an accident, while occipital fractures, particularly depressed occipital fractures are highly indicative of abuse. The site and cause of cranial fractures is shown in Table 3.3.

	Accident ($n = 60$)	Abuse ($n = 29$)
Parietal	57	27
Occipital	3	16
Frontal	0	4
Temporal	1	5
Anterior/middle cranial fossae	1	4

Table 3.3.   Site and extent of cranial injuries (Hobbs 1984)

Subdural haematomas arise in over half of cases without the presence of a skull fracture. Hobbs (1993b) reports that for a while they were known as 'spontaneous subdural haematomas' until it was recognised that the children had been abused. They are usually caused by violent shaking which disrupts the bridging cerebral veins leading to bleeding into the subdural space, often over a wide area bilaterally.

In some cases the only other evidence may be retinal haemorrhage, and there may be no other injury or bruising to the baby. Children who develop irritability, vomiting, decreasing levels of consciousness, and irregular breathing or apnoea shortly after an alleged trivial head injury have probably been abused. The diagnosis is confirmed on computer tomography (CT) scan.

RETINAL HAEMORRHAGE

Retinal haemorrhages are one of the classic signs of the shaken baby syndrome, occurring in about 80 per cent of cases. They may occur in front of, within, or under the retina, and are usually bilateral. They frequently coexist with subdural haemorrhage, although the exact mechanism by which they occur is not clearly understood.

BURNS AND SCALDS

Accidental burns and scalds occur in children because of a lapse in the usual protection given to the child. Neglected children may be burnt because of inadequate or negligent parenting, which is a failure to protect the child, whereas in abused children burns and scalds are deliberately inflicted.

Burns and scalds within the range of child abuse are seen as serious injuries, as sadistic and linked with the sexual or violent arousal of an adult, and as punitive to evoke fear.

Facts and figures

Deliberate burns and scalds are found in:

- 10 per cent of physically abused children;

- 5 per cent of sexually abused children;

- 1–16 per cent of all children presenting in A&E with burns and scalds.

The peak age of children accidentally burning or scalding themselves is during the second year and the peak age of children being deliberately burned is during the third year (Hobbs 1993c).

Types of thermal injury

Scalds
Scalds are caused by hot water, e.g. in drinks, liquid food and baths. They cause blisters and the affected skin peels away in sheets and is soggy and blanched. Scalds have a characteristic shape: they follow the contours of clothes and are enhanced by them. Drip, pour and splash patterns may be seen. The depth of injury is variable and contoured.

Contact, dry burns
Such burns are caused by hot objects, usually metallic, and electric fires. The injury looks like a brand mark, sharply demarcated and with the shape of the object that caused it. The burn is dry and of uniform depth.

Burns from flames
These are caused by fires and matches and may be identified by charring and by singed hairs.

Cigarette burns
These leave a circular mark and a tail if the cigarette was brushed against the skin. In physical abuse the burn tends to form a crater and to scar because the injury is deep. The injury may be multiple but is not particularly common.

Electrical burns
These are small but deep with entry and exit points.

Friction burns

These occur when, for example, a child is dragged across a floor. Bony prominences are affected and the blisters are broken.

Chemical burns

These may cause staining and scarring of the skin.

Radiant burns

These are caused by radiant energy, for example, from a fire or the sun. Injury is usually extensive and affects one aspect of an arm, leg or the body and is limited by the clothing. The skin shows erythema and blistering. Such burns occur in children who are made to stand in front of a fire.

Burn sites in abuse

Non-accidental burns affect the face and head, perineum, buttocks and genitalia, the hands, feet and legs (Johnson, 1990).

Cigarette burns may be seen on the face and head. Burns from hot food may be seen around rather than in the mouth when food has been pushed into the face.

To punish wetting or soiling misdemeanours, abusing parents may dip the child's buttocks into a bath of hot water. Burns to the perineum and genitalia may also occur in sexual abuse.

Hands commonly show burns to the dorsal surface in physical abuse, whereas in accidents the palm is most commonly affected. Hands may be burnt by being held under a tap or against a hot object.

The soles of the feet may show contact or cigarette burns. Burns on the feet or ankles may show a stocking distribution with no splash marks and a clear tidemark when they have been caused by forced immersion in a sink or bath.

Accidental burns

Most common in toddlers and older infants when the child pulls kettles, pans or cups of hot water from a kitchen unit or table. The scald affects the face, shoulders, upper arms and upper trunk (Hobbs, 1993c).

Assessment of burns – accident or abuse?

- Does the history explain the extent, depth, pattern, type and age of injury?

- Is there a more likely explanation if the history doesn't fit?

- Is the burn compatible with the child's ability and development?

- Are there other injuries which may suggest abuse?

- Are there signs of sexual abuse, failure to thrive or neglect?

- Has the child given a history: in parent's presence? elsewhere?

- Have the parents responded reasonably to the injury and are they cooperating with treatment?

- Who is taking responsibility? Are the parents detached or lacking concern for the child?

- How is the child behaving? Is he withdrawn, frozen or hyperactive, anxious, or aggressive?

Points to remember

- Most burn and scald injuries occur in pre-school children and should be prevented.

- Burns and scalds following abuse are under-reported.

- Evaluation is difficult, requiring careful assessment and a detailed history. A visit to the home by the health visitor is often necessary.

- Significant points in the history are unwitnessed incidents, delayed presentation, minimisation of severity of the injury, surprising lack of pain, and repeated burns.

- There is a particular association between sexual abuse and burns.

- Burns may be associated with any form of abuse.

4

Sexual Abuse

DEFINITION

> The involvement of dependent, developmentally immature children and adolescents in sexual activities they do not truly comprehend, to which they are unable to give informed consent or that violate the social taboos of family roles.
> **Department of Health 1992**

Child sexual abuse includes intercourse or attempted intercourse, fondling/caressing and also exposing a child to overtly sexual acts within the home or community, or through media sources.

FACTS AND FIGURES

It is estimated that over 6600 children under the age of 16 years are sexually abused each year in England and Wales (NSPCC 1990).

Of these incidents 78 per cent involve female children and 22 per cent male children.

> We have learned during the Inquiry that sexual abuse occurs in children of all ages, including the very young, to boys as well as girls, in all classes of society and frequently within the privacy of the family.
> **Report of the Inquiry into Child Abuse in Cleveland 1987**
> **(Butler-Sloss 1988)**

PATTERNS OF ABUSE

The abuser is almost always a male known to the child. Child sexual abuse may occur in any section of society but is found more commonly in poor families. It occurs in a variety of situations:

Intrafamilial

Includes abuse within the nuclear and extended family and may involve family friends, lodgers or close acquaintances with the knowledge of the family. Abuse within adoptive or foster families is included here.

Extrafamilial

Frequently includes abuse by adults known to the child from a variety of sources such as neighbours, family friends, schoolfriends' parents, as well as abuse within 'sex rings'.

Institutional

Includes abuse occurring within schools, residential children's homes, day nurseries, holiday camps, for example, cubs, brownies, boy scouts and other organisations both secular and religious.

Street or stranger abuse

Includes assaults on children in public places and child abduction.

RISK FACTORS

There are five main risk factors which predispose to child sexual abuse:

1. Previous incest or sexual deviance in the family.

2. New male member of the household with a record of sexual offences.

3. Loss of inhibition due to alcohol.

4. Loss of maternal libido or sexual rejection of father.

5. A paedophilic sexual orientation, especially in relation to sex rings and pornography.

ESSENTIAL CHARACTERISTICS

- Children in general do not like it.

- Sexual gratification of the abuser is the usual aim of the abuse.

- There is a power/age differential which effectively removes meaningful consent.

- The activity is usually secretive, collusive and perpetuated by the more powerful person. However, sometimes the strong needs of the child for physical affection, attention and dependency lead to the child's apparent complicity or willingness to initiate and maintain the abuse (Hobbs et al, 1993).

ACCOMMODATION SYNDROME

When children are caught up in sexual abuse they develop an adjustment pattern which is known as accommodation syndrome. This syndrome was recognised by Summit in 1983. There are five characteristics of child sexual abuse accommodation.

Secrecy

The child is told not to tell. Threats of violence are common, as are promises of withdrawal of affection and love. Older children understand the implications of a police investigation: possible imprisonment of father, loss of income, shame and the possibility that they are to blame. All of these are usually enough to maintain a child's silence.

Helplessness

In most cases children are unable to stop the abuse. They may resist initially, but then find it easier to pretend to be asleep. In this way they attempt to protect themselves. Hobbs et al (1993) report that the cost the child pays for the abandonment of active resistance is insecurity, victimisation and a loss of psychological well-being. The child is helpless, powerless and has no-one to turn to.

Entrapment and accommodation

Children feel trapped and that there is no way out of the situation. They may feel that they are to blame and guilt is a feeling shared by sexually abused children. They may face other pressures:

- The need to protect other children. The abuser may threaten to start abusing other children, possibly younger siblings, if he is stopped from abusing the child concerned.

- The need to protect the other parent.

- The need to protect the family home and integrity of the family (Hobbs et al, 1993).

Delayed disclosure

Many children never disclose their sexual abuse, and disclosures that arise often do so by chance. Hanks et al (1988) reports that there is no particular age when disclosure is more common.

Retraction

When children and even adults report sexual abuse, there is a strong likelihood that they will retract the allegations under pressure. This retraction reassures, encourages disbelief of the original disclosure and may lead to inaction (Hobbs et al, 1993). Goodwin (1989) states that 'people are happier to believe that children lie than that they are sexually abused'.

FACTS ABOUT ABUSERS

- Most abusers are known to the child.

- Most abusers commit large numbers of offences involving large numbers of children.

- The majority of abusers start behaving in this way as adolescents.

- Many abusers report sexual abuse themselves as children, but not all. They do, however, report difficult and damaging experiences as children.

Wolf (1988) looked into convicted abuser's childhood experiences and found that:

- 17 per cent witnessed sexual abuse;

- 23 per cent were victims of emotional abuse;

- 27 per cent were victims of sexual abuse;

- 30 per cent were victims of violence;

- 37 per cent had witnessed violence.

> Child sexual abusers include white-collar workers, priests, doctors, attorneys, judges, blue-collar workers and those who have no job.
> **Wolf, 1988**

TYPES OF SEXUAL ABUSE

Two types of sexual abuse can occur:

Contact

- Touching, fondling or oral contact with breasts or genitals.

- Insertion of fingers or objects into vulva or anus.

- Masturbation: by adult of him/herself in the presence of the child, including ejaculation onto the child; by adult of child or by child of adult.

- Intercourse: vaginal, anal or oral intercourse whether actual or attempted in any degree. This is usually with the adult as the active party but in some cases a child may be encouraged to penetrate the adult.

- Rape is attempted/achieved penile penetration of the vagina.

- Other genital contact; intracrural intercourse where the penis is laid between the legs, or genital contact with any part of the child's body, for example, rubbed penis on the child's thigh.

- Prostitution: any of the above abuse which includes the exchange of money, gifts or favours and applies to both boys ('rent boys') or girls.

Non-contact

- Exhibitionism (flashing).

- Pornography of many kinds; photographing sexual acts or anatomy.

- Showing pornographic photographs, films or videos.

- Erotic talk, telling children titillating or sexually explicit stories.

- Other sexual exploitations, sadistic activities.

- Burning a child's buttocks or genital area (Hobbs et al. 1993).

BROAD ASPECTS OF EFFECTS

Short-term: Child

- Emotional and behavioural effects.

- Educational and learning.

- Social relationships.

Hobbs et al. (1993) report that children may exhibit disturbed behaviour, for example, soiling, bed-wetting, self-injury or abnormal emotional states such as anxiety, depression and withdrawal. They may have difficulty with learning and require special assistance. Their relationships with adults and other children may be distorted in that they may have no friends, or alienate themselves by involving other children in sexual activities.

Long-term: Adult

- Mental health problems: depression, suicide, self-injury, poor self-esteem, alcohol and/or drug abuse.

- Sexual adjustment difficulties: prostitution, marital difficulties, aversion to sexual contact, fertility control.

- Child-tearing difficulties: repeated cycles of abuse, over-protectiveness, fear of closeness.

- Social dysfunction: delinquency, criminal behaviour/offending, and acts of violence (Hobbs et al. 1993).

Kitzinger (1990) reports that female survivors of child sexual abuse often have overwhelming memories of the abuse during medical procedures. A fear of and resistance to internal examinations while in the powerless position of a patient is a 'trade mark' previously abused women share. For some, the fear of being examined means they avoid attending for internal examinations such as during screening and antenatal care.

FACTORS WHICH AFFECT OUTCOME IN CHILD SEXUAL ABUSE

Type of sex act

Penetrative abuse is considered more harmful than non-penetrative (Russell 1986). This is also reflected in the way the law views the seriousness of various offences, for example, in rape cases.

Frequency and duration

The view is that harmfulness is related to frequency and duration. Long-term abuse is likely to lead to accommodation which may be associated with fewer symptoms in the short term but it may be associated with greater long-term psychological harm.

Degree of force and violence

Society sees physical force or violence as abusive, whereas subtle inducements, even though the outcome may be the same, are often not viewed in the same way. However, whilst force is initially traumatising there may be some solace for the victim who is able to perceive later the wrongfulness of the experience and his/her lack of involvement. Children who are tricked, bribed or seduced to comply may feel complicity and their view of themselves may be distorted. (Hobbs et al. 1993).

Relationship with offender

Abuse by close relatives, especially a parent figure, is thought to be most harmful (Russell 1986) although no connection between the closeness of the relationship and the effect on the child has been established. The quality of other non-abusing relationships will also influence the outcome.

Age of child

It is often thought that pre-school children who do not understand the wrongfulness of the act will suffer less harm. However, many young children show signs of emotional disturbance, indicating that although they may not fully comprehend what is right or wrong in what they have experienced, negative effects have been perceived and responses have occurred. The development of trust may be harmed and relationships become distorted. Adolescents are especially vulnerable – they are at the age where they are searching for identity and understanding of normal and deviant sexual relationships. Guilt is common and may be compounded by the pleasurable effects which may sometimes be felt from the sexual contact. Age is a vital factor and different effects are expressed at different developmental stages. Hanks et al. (1988) describe the significance of this complex factor:

> Sexual abuse strikes at the foundation of the child's development as an individual. Abuse occurring in the early stage of a child's life (from birth to five years of age) is more likely to lead to major and fundamental changes in normal development and from what we have seen so far to have life-long consequences. These children have been deprived of trust and security within a relationship. What is more they have come to regard human relationships in a distorted way – a distortion that they are at first not aware of and that cumulatively grows. As they grow older and reach the age of around nine years they become clearly aware of the taboo which exists about incest and withdraw in shame and guilt, or turn to aggressive or abusive behaviour themselves.

Multiple abusers

The child that is abused by multiple abusers tends to believe that the blame for the abuse lies with him/herself rather than with the offenders and the harmful effects are, therefore, compounded.

Effects of disclosure

Denial or disbelief by someone in a position of responsibility, for example mother or father, is a major source of harm to the child already suffering sexual abuse, as it adds to the child's sense of betrayal. Even when the disclosure is believed the effects on the family can be traumatic – break-up of relationships, suicide and emotional turmoil are all harmful, and many children receive little in the way of therapeutic help. As Frothingham et al (1991) report, the attitude is often to 'forget about it as quickly as possible'. The long-term outcome is affected by the child successfully revealing the abuse, being believed and being protected.

LONG-TERM EFFECTS OF CHILD SEXUAL ABUSE ADAPTED TO MASLOW'S HUMAN NEEDS

Self-actualization

Loss of motivation

Inability to plan for future

Phobias/aversions

Aesthetic need

Promiscuity

Oversexualisation

Sexual dissatisfaction

Sexual orientation crisis

Vaginismus

Anorgasmia

Amenorrhoea

Cognitive needs

Cognitive distortions

Denial

Dissociation

Nightmares

Hallucinations (tactile)

Perceptual delusions

Educational deficits

Esteem needs

Anxiety

Low self-image

Guilt

Worthlessness

Hopelessness

Acceptance and belonging

Isolation from others

Social withdrawal

Difficulty in establishing relationships

Gender conflict

Safety and security

Anger

Self-mutilation

Suicide

Revictimisation

Sleep disturbance

Inability to separate sex from affection

Physiological needs

Loss of weight

Substance abuse

Amnesia

Anorexia nevosa.

(Gillespie, 1993)

DISCLOSURE OF CHILD SEXUAL ABUSE

Why should we believe a child?

1. The more detail that is recalled, the more likely it is to be true.

2. Do the core elements of the story remain consistent?

3. Distinguishing details, for example, taste or smell of semen, are not learned from watching sexually explicit material on television or videos.

4. Children are known to recall events accurately from the preverbal stage of development.

5. Children's memory is no less accurate than adults, but children tend to recall less detail. Children relate events within the limits of their language and understanding.

6. Children can place events in correct temporal order.

7. Recantations are uncommon, stereotyped and often use incongruous language.

8. Children may be silenced by fear, coercion or anxiety.

9. Children cannot fantasize sexual acts of which they have no experience (Hobbs et al. 1993).

PHYSICAL EVIDENCE

In child sexual abuse, genital and anal examination should be in the context of a general clinical examination and include a search for other forms of abuse and an appraisal of growth, development and health. The behaviour of the child in front of the parents should be noted.

It is important to remember that many sexually abused children show no physical signs. Masturbation, oral sex and vaginal intercourse with a teenager may leave no mark. Wynne (1988) found that only 16 per cent of children had been anally abused, but this is more common in older boys and younger children. (Buggery is anatomically possible with a one-year-old child but vaginal intercourse does not become possible until a girl is aged seven or eight). Even when there were cases of anal abuse, less than half showed reflex anal dilatation.

Even when signs believed to be indicative of sexual abuse present, the diagnosis should very rarely be made on these alone. Confirmation depends on a multidisciplinary investigation. As Robinson (1991) writes, the most important single feature is a statement by the child; this may be supported by medical and forensic evidence, an admission by the abuser, and comprehensive assessment of the child, family and social background.

A summary of the role of medical staff at initial contact with an abused child is summarised in Figure 1.

WHY SHOULD THE GENITALIA BE EXAMINED?

The genitalia should be examined in child sexual abuse for five reasons:

1. To detect traumatic or infective conditions that may require treatment.

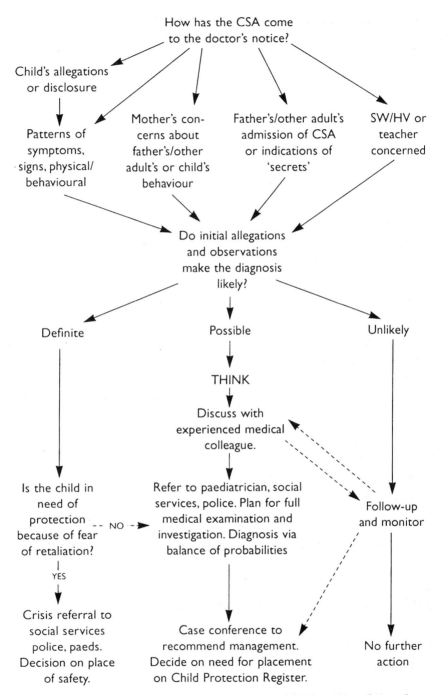

Figure 4.1. The initial medical contact's role. Taken from: *Diagnosis of Child Sexual Abuse: Guidance for Doctors*, 1988

2. To evaluate the nature of any abuse. Normal genital and anal appearances do not exclude the diagnosis, but in young children they make penetrative abuse unlikely.

3. To provide forensic evidence that may be helpful to the future protection of children.

4. To reassure the child, who sometimes feels that serious damage has been done.

5. To start the process of recovery (Bamford and Roberts 1993).

SIGNS OF INTERCRURAL INTERCOURSE

There are usually no signs of intercrural intercourse but occasionally bruising of the perineum may occur. There may be redness of the labia and perineum, but this is common in other conditions, such as poor hygiene. There may be a split in the posterior fourchette and a subsequent scar.

SIGNS OF BUGGERY

The signs of buggery are likely to be most prominent in younger children. In most cases there may be no abnormal signs; however, signs to look out for include the following:

External trauma in anal abuse

- Fissures due to overstretching of the sphincter are often multiple and they radiate. Their extent is in proportion to the disparity in size between the abuser and the child and the degree of force used. They may leave scars or anal tags.

- Swelling of the skin around the anal verge may be seen after recent abuse and thickening after repeated abuse.

- Perineal bruising or bleeding without reasonable explanation is highly suspicious.

- Warts around the anus (or vagina) may be transmitted by genital contact and are strongly indicative of sexual abuse, especially if a wart virus of a genitally transmitted type is identified.

Anal dilatation

Given that the bowel is normal and the child does not suffer from any neurological disorder, abnormal patency is indicative of something hard and large having passed through the anus. 'Reflex' anal dilatation is not a true reflex and amounts to relaxation of the anal sphincter about 10 seconds after the anus has been inspected so that an initially closed anus opens during examination. The argument, as Robinson (1991) recognises, is whether this is a sign of repeated anal penetration or whether it occurs normally or as a result of conditions such as chronic constipation and Crohn's disease.

SIGNS ASSOCIATED WITH SEXUAL ABUSE

1. Bruising, abrasions, reddening, oedema of external and internal genitalia.

2. Recent or healing lacerations of labia, posterior fourchette.

3. Lacerations or scars on hymen which may extend to posterior vaginal wall.*

4. Dilated hymenal opening.

5. Attenuated hymen with loss of hymenal tissue.*

6. Multiple healed hymenal tears seen as clefts or rounded remnants (congenital variants).

7. Sexually transmitted disease.*

8. Vulvovaginitis (not sexually transmitted).

9. Dilated and/or traumatised urethra.

10. Labial fusion, of variable degree (usually posterior).

11. Scars, e.g. at the posterior fourchette or in the vaginal wall.*

12. Remember to look for signs of:
   other physical abuse
   anal/oral abuse
   self-mutilation
   eating disorder

13. Pregnancy.

Note: Signs marked * are highly indicative of abuse and in some instances diagnostic (Hobbs et al. 1993).

DIFFERENTIAL DIAGNOSIS OF SEXUAL ABUSE

1. Accidental trauma.

2. Skin disorder, e.g. atopic eczema.

3. Congenital abnormality, e.g. midline raphe, wedge-shaped area in midline.

4. Infection, e.g. candidiasis, streptococcal cellulitis.

5. Inflammatory bowel disease, e.g. Crohn's disease.

6. Severe, chronic constipation causing anal laxity.

7. Single anal fissure, e.g. constipation.

8. Neurological disorder, e.g. neurogenic bowel in association with spina bifida.

9. Rectal tumour (Hobbs et al. 1993).

SEXUAL ABUSE COMBINED WITH PHYSICAL ABUSE

Hobbs and Wynne (1993) have found that physical abuse and child sexual abuse are closely related. They reported that one in seven sexually abused children had also been physically abused. The injuries may be like those seen in physical assault, but there are patterns associated with child sexual abuse:

- Grip marks on the inner aspect of the upper arms, thighs and around the knees.

- Petechiae around the orbit and linear marks around the neck, presumably in an attempt to quieten the child, the abuser puts a hand over the child's mouth.

- Bruises on the lower abdomen, particularly over the pubis and around the hips where the child has been grasped.

- 'Love-bites' whatever the age of the child, on the neck, breasts, back and shoulders.

- Burns and scalds are one of the least recognised manifestations of abuse and clinical assessment may be difficult.

HIV INFECTION

The realisation is slowly beginning to dawn on health care professionals that, as well as the emotional, psychological and physical damage caused by child sexual abuse, there is the possibility that the child may have been infected with HIV. HIV infection has been recognised in child sexual abuse and the cases due to sexual assault are likely to rise (Gellert 1989). Testing for HIV needs careful consideration, but the following guidelines could apply:

- If a child is unwell with signs and symptoms of the HIV infection, he should be tested.

- If a child has been involved in high risk activities, e.g. prostitution or drug abuse, he should probably be tested.

- If a child (usually a teenager) insists on being tested, this needs careful consideration. Francis (1993), believes that the perpetrator should be tested first.

- A single act of stranger abuse, a coexistent sexually transmitted disease, previous anal or oral abuse do not currently warrant screening.

- Counselling for the child and his/her carers is mandatory. (Hobbs et al. 1993)

POINTS TO REMEMBER

- Doctors examining children where child sexual abuse is suspected should not work in isolation, but recognise the need for multidisciplinary teamwork.

- Consent is needed before any examination.

- The diagnosis of child sexual abuse is made by building up the pieces of the diagnostic jigsaw: the medical examination is just one part of this process.

- Children's disclosures of abuse should initially be accepted.

- Physical indicators of child sexual abuse are important because they may be the first sign of child abuse. They also corroborate the child's story.

- Normal physical examination is common even when a child has been a victim of child sexual abuse.

- Single physical signs may support the diagnosis of child sexual abuse but are rarely proof of its existence. Pregnancy, gonorrhoea or the presence of sperm in the vagina or rectum are the exceptions to this.

- Physical abuse and child sexual abuse are seen together in approximately 15 per cent of cases. Burns and bites are particularly associated with child sexual abuse.

- All sexually abused children have been emotionally abused.
(Hobbs et al. 1993).

5

Emotional Abuse

DEFINITION

The severe adverse effect on the behaviour and emotional development of
a child caused by persistent or severe emotional ill-treatment: this category
should be used when it is the sole form of abuse.
Department of Health 1992

Emotional abuse is probably the most common type of abuse and can take
many forms:

- lack of care for physical needs;

- failure to provide constant love and affection;

- overt hostility and rejection.

All abuse entails some emotional ill treatment.
D Skuse 1993

FACTS AND FIGURES

In 1988 one in eight children on the child protection register had suffered
neglect or emotional abuse.

Despite being the most common form of abuse it is rarely the sole
reason for seeking child protection through legal proceedings.

IDENTIFICATION

Observing emotional abuse is very difficult as it is normally hidden and carried out in private. Although direct observation of parenting may raise suspicion, the diagnosis is usually made by the effect on the child in terms of emotional, physical or behavioural growth. Symptoms that are suspicious may not be indicative of abuse or neglect, but it is important to recognise that the cessation of emotional abuse by placing a child in an alternative family is followed by rapid and dramatic improvement. In this instance the diagnosis is usually made in retrospect.

Garbarino et al (1988) identified five components important in assessing emotional ill treatment. These components are useful in looking at a child's behaviour in relation to the type of abuse they have been suffering. These range from mild through moderate and severe.

- **Rejecting** – the adult refuses to acknowledge the child's worth and needs.

- **Isolating** – the adult cuts the child off from normal social experiences and contacts and prevents the child from forming friendships, making the child feel he is alone in the world.

- **Terrorising** – the adult verbally assaults the child, creates a climate of fear and bullies and frightens the child.

- **Ignoring** – the adult deprives the child of essential stimulation and responsiveness, stifling emotional growth and development.

- **Corrupting** – the adult 'mis-socialises' the child, stimulating the child to engage in destructive antisocial behaviour, reinforcing deviance which makes the child unfit for normal social experiences.

By looking at these five categories of emotional maltreatment, an idea can be gained as to how parents behave towards their child. Children's reactions vary as to the degree of abuse. Also, depending on the age of the child, his or her development will be affected. Spitz (1948) states that it is clear that the emotional care of the very young child is important and that infants need an emotionally rich environment to function and grow appropriately. Infants and children who grow up lacking physical care and nurturance at every level will suffer in the short term and long term.

This manifests in different ways from total withdrawal to more active disturbances such as hostility and aggression. Infants who have been abused may show an over-anxious attachment, their lack of security does not allow them to explore their surroundings. They will seem ill at ease, whining, unhappy and cling to their carer who responds with irritation. Alternatively, there may be little evidence of any attachment behaviour. The child either roams around the room in a completely nondirected fashion due to high anxiety. Or they may creep into a corner and watch the proceedings warily. This behaviour is termed 'frozen watchfulness'.

Neglect

DEFINITION

The persistent or severe neglect of a child (for example by exposing to any kind of danger, including cold and starvation) which results in serious impairment of the child's health or development, including non-organic failure to thrive.
Department of Health 1992

FACTS AND FIGURES

The true number of children reported and registered as suffering from neglect is difficult to ascertain. The figure that is reported is only the tip of the iceberg.

Helfer (1990) wrote of increasing 'de-emphasis' on the neglect of children whereby even professionals mandated to report neglect may not do so, feeling that nothing will (or can) be done by overwhelmed under-resourced child protection agencies.

Creighton and Noyes (1990) found that:

- 13 per cent of children registered were registered because of neglect.

- 2 per cent of children were registered because of neglect and physical abuse.

- The average age of children registered as a result of neglect was four years nine months.

Department of Health figures show that in March, 1991:

- 12 per cent of children were registered because of neglect.

- 40 per cent were suspected as being abused and the cause was recorded as grave concern, of these 7 per cent was due to neglect, 2 per cent emotional abuse and 1 per cent failure to thrive.

The NSPCC (1990) reported on the social status of children with neglect:

- Only 15 per cent of mothers and 39 per cent of fathers were in paid employment, mostly semi-skilled and unskilled manual jobs.

- Marital problems were the commonest cause of stress in 30 per cent and debt was a factor in 22 per cent of families.

- 38 per cent of children registered were living with their mother alone.

The physical manifestations and consequences of neglect are shown in Table 5.1.

INDICATIONS OF NEGLECT

- The child is not attached or is anxiously attached to the parent. There is lack of emotional nurturance for emotional growth (emotional neglect).

- The child is undernourished because the parents have not fed him available food (non-organic failure to thrive).

- The child is unattended and in unsafe circumstances (supervision neglect).

- The child is placed, either by omission or commission by the parent, in situations of unnecessary risk for emotional or physical harm.

- As a result of a deficit in stimulation, the child is developmentally delayed, especially in language and social development, or social development is aberrant. There is lack of age-appropriate and consistant limit setting.

- The child is not given necessary medication or treatment to control a chronic disease, or medical care is inadequately provided for acute illnesses and well child care (Cantwell and Rosenberg 1993).

Deprivation	Result
Supervision, safe environment	Accidents – falls, scalds, ingestions, road traffic accidents, house fires, drowning
Lack of seatbelt	Accidents
Medical care – • Fail to immunise • Fail to seek advice • Fail to attend for development checks • Refusal of medical care	Measles, rubella, mumps, whooping cough, etc. Illness recognised when child seriously ill/dying Squint, deafness, other disorders not recognised Prolonged illness, avoidable complication, death
Hygiene in the home	Repeated episodes of gastroenteritis, skin infections, head lice
Clean air	Dirty child, infection, especially respiratory, asthma
Warmth	Cold injury – red swollen hands and feet, hypothermia, infection, especially chest/pneumonia
Food	Malnourished – small, thin, may be stunted 'emotional dwarf', with apparently adequate nutrition, impaired brain growth (especially less than 2 years), vitamin deficiency, failure to thrive
Drink	Inappropriate patterns of drinking, e.g. from toilet or drains – causing gastrointestinal infections
Physical care	Dry, thin, sparse hair, alopecia, cradle cap, nappy rash, spotty skin, maceration in skin folds. Thickened yellow nails. Dirty, smelly body with infestations, e.g. head lice. Vulvovaginitis, especially in young girls. Clothing inappropriate, inadequate, dirty

Table 5.1   Physical manifestations/consequences of neglect (Hobbs et al, 1993)

POINTS TO CONSIDER

- Neglect is insidious and a prevalent form of maltreatment.

- It affects children in many ways from poor health to developmental delays.

- Neglected children may also be abused in other ways.

- Most of the children who are reported as neglected are under five years of age, but it continues through childhood.

- Parents may have little awareness of their own inadequacies in child rearing and the longer neglect continues the more difficult it is to help children more effectively.

- Neglected children are at risk of growing up to be adults with limited skills in all sorts of areas and of becoming inadequate, neglectful parents.

- Neglecting families have a poor prognosis for change – the earlier the intervention the greater the chance for progress.

- Preventable accidents are a major cause of morbidity and mortality in neglectful families. The significance of repeated accidents should be recognised in the A&E department (Hobbs et al. 1993).

CASE STUDIES

Case 1

A baby aged six months was found dead in his cot. He was very thin, had numerous bruises on his chest and back, scratches on his face and he was dirty with severe nappy rash. Two further children were subsequently born to this family. They were severely neglected and care orders were made at the age of two and one years.

Following the death of the first child an autopsy report commented on the poor growth and superficial injuries of the baby. No cause of death was found. The parents were reassured and told 'they had nothing to reproach themselves for'.

Case 2

A 4-year-old boy was found dead in bed. He had had measles and an autopsy showed he had died of bronchopneumonia. The family were well known to professional agencies. The boy had 'failed to thrive', and was not immunised. The family had recently moved into temporary housing known to be cold, with a leaking roof. They were not registered with a general practitioner and when the emergency doctor service arrived it was too late. It was Christmas Day.

Death was recorded as due to 'natural causes'.

Case 3

A single mother and her children aged three and one years lived in sheltered housing. The mother was very independent and known to be 'difficult'. She had a past history of drug abuse but was not currently abusing drugs or alcohol. Her three older children were in the care of their father. When the younger child became ill his mother said that the doctor was not needed. Three days later his mother arrived screaming at the warden's office that her son was dead. He died in the ambulance. Autopsy showed that the 14 month old child had died of septicaemia secondary to otitis media.

Case 4

Four-year-old twins were playing on the railway line. Their mother had left them for the afternoon with their father and his partner, neither of whom wished to share care of the boys. One boy was hit by the footplate of a passing express train and killed. The Coroner commented on the need for British Rail to keep their fences in better repair.

The above deaths were due to neglect but were neither recognised nor recorded (Hobbs et al, 1993).

Failure to Thrive

Abuse and neglect may have an adverse effect on a child's physical growth. When this manifests in infancy, the main effect is on weight gain. The phrase 'failure to thrive' refers to children who are growth retarded secondary to malnutrition. The term was first used to describe infants living in institutions or hospitals; these infants were sad and pathetic creatures (Spitz 1945). Failure to thrive can be broken down into **organic failure to thrive** and **non-organic failure to thrive**. In the case of children who are victims of abuse or neglect, an organic cause is usually ruled out.

Failure to thrive occurs when an infant or child fails to achieve the expected growth as assessed by height and weight. It is a symptom that presents where there may be no other evidence of abuse. The key to diagnosis is a good history. Failure to recognise this condition may have consequences for a child's future physical development, intelligence, social adjustment and emotional well-being.

DEFINITIONS

Non-organic failure to thrive is related to maternal rejection and deprivation. It arises from an insufficiently nurturing environment in the home or environment.
Fischhoff 1975

Failure to thrive is the child who refuses to gain weight in the approved manner.
Illingworth 1983

Much failure to thrive is nutritional neglect and results from feeding an infant inadequate calories – either simply not enough food or a bizarre diet. It leads to failure to thrive, a potentially life-threatening condition in which the child's weight, height and often head circumference fall below the third centile of children his age.
Kempe and Kempe 1978

Many definitions are to be found on this subject but the same characteristics apply – all infants are below their estimated weight and this is due to inadequate nutrition. It is the reason for the inadequate nutrition that counts. In abused children the reason may be that food is withheld or the diet is sporadic. The environment the child is brought up in may be hostile and so children will not eat.

PARENTS' BEHAVIOUR

Parents may present as:

- stressed;
- depressed;
- in ill health themselves;
- having eating problems;
- having difficulties in parenting;
- having suffered maternal rejection;
- having distorted and unrealistic expectations of the child;
- lacking in knowledge about child care;
- neglectful of themselves and children;
- too poor to have adequate food in the house.

In the A&E department it is important to look at the whole child. This includes the interaction with the parents; parents who abuse their children emotionally will carry this into the department. Some parents will see their behaviour as normal, due to various factors such as the way they were brought up and the way they were taught to parent. When assessing a child look at their size in accordance with their weight, if the presenting injury/illness is suspicious or cause for concern then the fact the child is also extremely underweight may give more information as to whether it was as a result of a non-accidental injury.

CASE STUDIES

Case 1

After seeing a four-year-old girl who was failing to thrive for some months without improvement it was decided to visit the child's home and observe her feeding. She was the middle child of five and her other four sisters appeared to be thriving well. The children ate in the kitchen, the food was distributed by the father and then eaten alone, with the parents sitting apart in another room.

The food was distributed in quantity according to a well-established formula which the father knew and could explain. The oldest child, aged 9, received the most, about 3 times as much as the child who was failing to thrive. The other children, including a two-year-old also received more than her. The father explained that it was pointless to give her more food because she would not eat it and it would probably end up on one of the other children's plates. The child confirmed the father's prediction and ate very little in comparison with her sisters.

Case 2

A boy of 15 months had been failing to thrive from about four months of age. He had had many infectious illnesses including bacterial meningitis but it was felt that his failure to thrive was primarily the result of inadequate feeding. His mother was a slim unsupported single parent who negated most of the advice which had been offered, predicting that nothing would work. She said that he usually refused much of what was given to him.

A feeding session was arranged in the home. The child was fed a large bowl of stew by spoon, initially with him standing holding a toy. He started to refuse but his mother held him tightly and encouraged him, eventually giving him a good sized portion. Towards the end it was apparent both she and the child were more relaxed and she interacted in a warm and encouraging way with him. On viewing the film later, it was noticed that steam was rising from the food and it could be seen quite clearly that the child pulled back at the first mouthfuls of food that touched his mouth. The mother said she did not want to see the film but the temperature was discussed. Shortly after, the child improved dramatically with a long period of weight gain.

(Hobbs et al, 1993)

6

Munchausen's Syndrome By Proxy

In 1951 Asher described a disorder in which adults described fabricated illnesses. Baron von Munchausen was born in 1720 and Dr Asher chose to dedicate the syndrome in memory of him as his patients also had characteristics of having travelled widely and the Baron's adventures also bore little semblance to reality. Since then, Munchausen's syndrome has become well recognised. In 1977 Meadow described Munchausen's syndrome by proxy in which a six-year-old girl presented with apparent haematuria. 'By proxy' means the parent (usually the mother) provides false information.

DEFINITION

Munchausen's syndrome by proxy includes the following:

- Illness in a child which is faked and/or produced by the parent or carer.

- Presentation of the child for medical assessment and care, usually persistently and resulting in multiple medical procedures and multiple medical opinions.

- Denial of knowledge by the perpetrator of the cause of the child's illness

- Acute symptoms and signs in the child abate when the child is separated from the perpetrator, although sequelae of the disorder may persist (Rosenberg 1987).

The child is abused in that the parent has feigned an illness and by their direct actions, i.e. the giving of drugs to induce symptoms. Also because the child has to undergo unnecessary investigations and treatment at the perpetrator's insistance.

The abuse manifests itself in four main ways.

PERCEIVED ILLNESS

Anxious parents worry needlessly that their child is ill. An inexperienced mother is more likely to perceive symptoms that others cannot see. The child is taken to doctors, sometimes on many occasions, when she cannot be reassured. Often they will insist on investigations and treatments.

DOCTOR SHOPPING

Some parents shop around or seek help from several different doctors. This may be done privately or within the NHS. They insist that their healthy child is ill and as each doctor refuses further investigation so they consult yet another doctor. The result for the child is countless investigations and a body that has been irradiated and biopsied.

ENFORCED INVALIDISM

Some parents who have an ill or disabled child seek to keep the child ill, increase the degree of disability or ensure the child is regarded as incapacitated. The parents of a child with spelling difficulties may insist their child is mentally disabled. The child is brought up to believe that he or she is ill and school attendance suffers. The parents of a child who has a disability may convince local authorities that the disability from the child's illness is greater than it is, and attendance at a special school may be arranged.

These types of behaviour are extensions of the usual way many parents behave when their child is ill. As with all forms of abuse it is the degree that matters. For a worried parent to seek a second or third opinion is reasonable, for them to seek a twenty-second opinion is excessive. It is parents who display these types of behaviour, who are unreasonable and cannot be dissuaded by careful and sympathetic help, that are causing abuse.

FABRICATED ILLNESS

Some parents lie to the doctor about their child's health and fabricate physical signs or alter health records. The child is usually young; abuse generally starts within the first two years of life. Parents may continue and intensify the child's illness as the years pass. If the abuse is not discovered before the child reaches school age then some children will participate in the deception. Signs and causes of fabricated symptoms are shown in Table 6.1.

There are five main consequences for the child who is labelled as ill:

- They receive needless and harmful investigations and treatments.

- A genuine disease may be induced by the abuser's actions – i.e. renal failure as a result of repeated injections of immunisation agents to cause fever.

- They may die suddenly as a result of the mother misjudging the degree of insult. Mothers who partially smother their children to cause unconsciousness may smother the child for too long thereby causing brain damage or death.

- They may develop chronic invalidism. The child may accept the illness story and believe himself to be disabled and unable to attend school, work or even to walk.

- They may develop Munchausen's syndrome as an adult – the children have learned and then taken over the lying behaviour of their mother. All children are victims of emotional abuse as a result (Meadow 1993).

WARNING SIGNS

- Persistent or recurrent illness that is unexplained or extremely rare.

- Discrepancy between child's apparent good health and history of grave symptoms or seriously disordered laboratory tests.

False sign	Cause
Seizures, apnoea drowsiness	Poisons, suffocation, pressure on neck
Bleeding (haematuria)	Blood from mother (particularly from a vaginal tampon), raw meat, or from child, added to sample from child or smeared around child's nose, vulva etc. Colouring agents added to sample or smeared on to child Warfarin administration
Fever	Warming thermometer, altering temperature chart Injections of contaminated material into child's vein, repetitive injections of antigenic material
Diarrhoea and vomiting	Laxatives Mechanically induced Salt induced or emetic poisoning
Hypertension	Altering blood pressure chart or instructions on size of cuff
Rashes	Scratching the skin to cause blisters Caustics and dyes
Renal stones	Addition of stone to child's urine to which blood has previously been added
Faeculent vomits	Making child vomit and stirring in faeces
Failure to thrive and thinness	Withholding food If in hospital and child is parentally fed interfering with treatment and sucking back stomach contents through nasogastric tubes

Table 6.1   Fabricated illnesses (Meadow 1993)

- Overly attentive mother will not leave the child and appears surprisingly cheerful in face of grave clinical situation.

- Signs and symptoms settle on separation from mother.

- Routine treatment or medication never seems to work well.

- Several previous medical opinions – notes are lost (Wisslow 1990).

- In over half the families other siblings are suffering similar abuse or another variety of abuse; in a few families there has been unexplained death of other young children.

- Some of the victims will have genuine illness in addition to the superimposed false illness.

- Up to one third of these children will have, or have had, failure to thrive, non-accidental injury or neglect in addition to the fictitious illness abuse (Meadow 1993).

FEATURES OF THE ABUSER

- The perpetrator may be found in any socioeconomic classes.

- In nearly all the cases the mother is the deceiver, the father does not know what is going on. She is the more dominant person in the marriage and is normally more intelligent and capable than her husband.

- In a small minority of cases, less than 5 per cent, the father is the perpetrator and the more dominant person in the marriage.

- Often the mother has previous nursing or medical experience and may have a history of fabrication of illness in herself.

- The mothers have usually had a difficult childhood themselves and usually lacked love and respect from their own mothers; many have been abused themselves as children.

- They thrive on the attention from health care professionals and in the medical environment.

- There tends to be a poor relationship between the mother and father of the child; the fathers tend to be distant and are unaware of what is going on.

- Although mothers may have had contact with a psychiatrist in the past, it is unusual for them to have had previous mental illness or to be found to have an illness at the time of the abuse. (Meadow 1993, Hobbs et al. 1993, Crouse 1992)

MANAGEMENT

To be able to manage Munchausen's syndrome by proxy (MSBP) professionals have to recognise that it exists and that there is a considerable risk of mortality to the child. As in all cases of abuse, or suspected abuse, the child's safety is paramount. The recognition of MSBP must involve all health care professionals involved in the care of the child. The general practitioner and health visitor are important in providing background information about the family. The paediatrician must recognise that in 'rare' diseases MSBP could be the cause. The abuse can sometimes continue in hospital and staff involved in caring for the child need to be fully involved. The need for correct observation of the child is paramount. There needs to be a meeting of health care professionals early on to facilitate information gathering and ensure good communication between those involved. The degree of abuse involved needs to be assessed and if the child is at risk then he or she has to be protected. For the majority of cases the family can be helped. The parents need to be confronted with the diagnosis – reactions will vary and some parents will need psychiatric help – but most children will be able to stay within their families with good social work support and continuing medical surveillance. When treating families it should be remembered that siblings are at risk of abuse, and should also be examined and involved in long-term family work.

7

Fatal Abuse

Infanticide is a practice that has existed for years. It may have started with the disposal of unwanted children: either illegitimate children who may have brought disgrace on the family, or handicapped children who may have passed on their defects. Many more children died as a result of starvation and neglect as their families could not support the large numbers of children.

Now death from child abuse remains a major cause of childhood mortality. The true incidence of fatal abuse remains underestimated – a reason for this may be that if the circumstances surrounding an infant death are doubtful, the parents are given the benefit of the doubt because it is always tragic when a child dies and to confront the parents at such a time is extremely difficult.

FACTS AND FIGURES

Home Office statistics show that babies under one year have the highest risk of murder – rates of 68 per million. Children aged 1–5 are the safest group with less than 12 per million murdered.

Jobling (1976) wrote 'estimates of numbers of children who die each year from their injuries range from 100–750'. An analysis for classification of diseases from 1974 to 1983 revealed an average of 138 deaths per year and an additional 50 deaths where violence played a part, but death was recorded as from natural causes. NSPCC (1984) estimate that each week four children will die as a result of abuse or neglect.

> The possibility of hidden abuse when an infant is found dead should be considered
> **Hobbs et al, 1993**

PRESENTATION OF FATAL ABUSE

- Severely battered infant or child.

- Unexpected death where occult injury is found.

- Cot death presentation (death from asphyxiation).

- Neglect – child deliberately or passively left in dangerous situation, e.g. drowning, house fire.

- Deliberate poisoning.

- Recurrent unexplained deaths.

- Child death associated with sexual assault.

COT DEATH PRESENTATION

Sudden infant death syndrome (cot death)

This is the commonest category of death in Britain for infants aged under one year. The label is given when no cause of death is found in a previously well infant. It affects two per 1000 births and is commonest in the first five months of life. It happens to children who are previously well and who have had no episodes of apnoea or other unexplained illness. It is extremely rare for it to recur in families.

Suffocation

Death due to asphyxiation is the commonest cause. The abuser is usually the mother who uses the hand or rolled up material to cause airway obstruction.

Clinical features

- It happens to young children aged under three years but more commonly to infants under one year.

- It can present following an apnoeic episode at home.

- It can present as sudden unexplained death (cot death), or the child may be moribund then recover spontaneously following resuscitation.

Warning features

- Sudden unexplained deaths in siblings.

- 'Near miss' cot death presentation.

- An infant with cot death over the age of six months (outside the usual age range for sudden infant death syndrome).

- Excess of boys in sibling groups.

- Petechiae on face or mouth, bruises to neck in a minority.

- Recurring attacks that reveal little on investigation.

- Can be associated with Munchausen syndrome by proxy and physical abuse (Meadow 1993).

POISONING

Accidental poisoning

Accidental poisoning is very common in children; non-accidental poisoning is less common but more serious. Accidental poisoning commonly occurs in children between 2 and 4 years; this is because of their inquisitive nature. The reason for the ingestion of tablets is usually due to inadequate adult supervision. Accidents do happen but repeated ingestion should be looked at more closely, and deliberate poisoning considered. Repeated ingestion is almost certainly due to neglect if not deliberate. Parents will sometimes have poisoned the child; detection of this is paramount for the child. Motives vary and will overlap with parents who create false illnesses in their child – and will do so to gain attention for themselves. Other parents will do it out of spite to teach the child a lesson.

Points to consider

Is the poisoning due to neglect, is it deliberate or accidental?

- Toddlers aged 18 months to 3 years will explore, try and taste things they find. By 4 to 5 years they will know not to eat pills.

- Children aged 3 years and older are able to give a history and tell if they 'ate' grandpa's 'sweeties' or if mummy gave them to the child herself.

- Deliberate poisoning mainly occurs in children below the age of 2 years.

- Is the story plausible – child-proof containers are not child-proof but will delay access to contents, so if a child has eaten half the container then where were the parents? Is the 2 year old able to climb on top of the cupboard and open a foil wrapper?

- Less than 15 per cent of children who present to hospital because of accidental poisoning will develop symptoms and death is extremely rare.

Presentation

Children who have been poisoned will present in four main ways.

- The parent rushes the child to hospital claiming that the child has ingested a drug accidentally.

- The child presents with inexplicable symptoms and signs, usually of acute onset.

- The child presents with recurrent unexplained illnesses that have the features of poisoning (see Table 7.1). These sorts of patients overlap with those for whom parents create false illness (Munchausen's syndrome by proxy).

- The child may be moribund or dead when first seen (Meadow 1993).

In all cases check for other signs of abuse and for unexplained deaths.

Signs and Symptoms	Drug
Seizures and apnoea spells	Salt (sodium chloride), phenothiazines, tricyclic antidepressants, hydrocarbons
Hyperventilation	Salicylates, acids
Drowsiness and stupor	Hypnotics, insulin, aspirin, paracetamol, tricyclic antidepressants, phenothiazines, anticonvulsants, methadone, cannabis
Hallucinations	Atropine-like agents
Bizarre motor movements	Phenothiazines, metoclopramide, antihistamines
Vomiting	Emetics and many other drugs
Diarrhoea (with or without failure to thrive)	Laxatives, including magnesium hydroxide (milk of magnesia), phenolphthalein, salt
Haematemesis	Salicylates, iron
Ulcerated mouth	Corrosives
Thirst	Salt (with or without water deprivation)
Bizarre biochemical blood profile	Salt, insulin, salicylates, sodium bicarbonate

Table 7.1   Summary of signs and symptoms of poisoning (Meadow, 1993)

8

Management of Child Abuse

THE CHILDREN ACT 1989

Main principles

- The welfare of the child is the paramount consideration in court proceedings.

- Wherever possible, children should be brought up and cared for within their own families.

- **Children should be safe and be protected by effective intervention if they are in danger.**

- When dealing with children, courts should ensure that delay is avoided, and may only make an order if to do so is better than making no order at all.

- Children should be kept informed about what happens to them, and should participate when decisions are made about their future.

- Parents continue to have parental responsibility for their children, even when their children are no longer living with them. They should be kept informed about their children and participate when decisions are made about their children's future.

- Parents with children in need should be helped to bring up their children themselves.

- This help should be provided as a service to the child and his family, and should:

    be provided in partnership with the parents;

meet each child's identified needs;

be appropriate to the child's race, culture, religion and language;

be open to effective independent representations and complaints procedures;

draw upon effective partnership between the local authority and other agencies, including voluntary agencies (Department of Health 1989).

Child protection aspects

- The Act is comprehensive and consolidates earlier law dealing with children.

- It was implemented in October 1991.

- The upbringing of children is primarily the responsibility of parents.

- A balance between child protection and minimal interference in family life is sought.

- Child protection is improved by the introduction of Child Assessment Orders and lower threshold for Emergency Protection Orders.

- An Emergency Protection Order may be challenged in court after 72 hours by parents.

- The child's welfare is 'paramount'.

- A court order should not be made unless it is better for the child than not making an order.

- A timetable will be set by the court to avoid delay.

The Act offers a new framework for the care and protection of children. It introduces new guidelines for use when children are at risk of **significant harm**. Under the Children Act, harm is defined as 'ill-treatment or impairment of health or development'. Ill-treatment may be physical, sexual or emotional (Hobbs et al, 1993).

Medical examination and assessment

With regards to non-emergency treatment, consent will be required from a person having parental responsibility for the child, or from the child if he or she is competent to make a medical decision. Such competence depends on age, intelligence, understanding and the information given. Examinations carried out without such consent could constitute assault. Where emergency treatment is required, the practitioner must rely on his own clinical judgement if those in a position to give consent are unavailable.

The child's right of refusal

The child may make an informed decision to refuse examination or assessment. This will depend on the age of the child, his or her understanding and whether information given has been sufficient.

Emergency Protection Orders

Emergency Protection Orders may be made if there is reasonable cause to believe the child may suffer significant harm unless:

- He is removed from where he is to another place;

- He is kept where he is;

- The parents unreasonably withhold access to the child and there is reason to believe that access is required as a matter of urgency.

The order may last for 8 days and can be extended once for a period of 7 days. It may be challenged at 72 hours by the parents if they were not present at the initial hearing.

Any person may apply to the court for an Emergency Protection Order if they are worried about a child's safety.

Child Assessment Order

A child Assessment Order can be used when the parents are uncooperative and there is a need to decide whether significant harm is likely but there is not an emergency. Notice is given so that all sides can be represented. If made, the order lasts for 7 days.

- Ill-treatment of the child is sufficient in itself to satisfy the criteria.

- It is not necessary to show that impairment of health or development follows the ill-treatment.

- It may be important to identify who ill-treated the child – did the carer harm the child or fail to prevent harm?

- Impairment of development includes physical, intellectual, emotional or behavioural development.

- The care expected may not be of a lower standard because the parents are unintelligent, alcoholic, drug users or otherwise disadvantaged.

Hobbs (1991) reports that the severity of the injury does not necessarily correlate with the seriousness of the harm. An abused child may not grow, develop intellectually or learn to love. Harm and abuse may well be hidden, particularly in child sexual abuse. It is vital that the harm from abuse is balanced with the effect of an intervention in the family.

CHILD PROTECTION TEAM

When dealing with suspected cases of abuse one area of contact in the management is the child protection team (CPT).

This is a team within the police force that specialises in child abuse and protection. With management of these cases a multidisciplinary approach is important to ensure the best action is taken for the child. For this purpose the CPT work closely with hospital staff, social services and carers.

Role of the CPT

Police involvement in cases of child abuse stems from their primary responsibilities to protect the community and to bring offenders to justice.

Their overriding consideration is the **welfare of the child**.

Police focus

- To determine whether a criminal offence has been committed.

- To identify the person(s) responsible.

- To secure the best possible evidence, in order that consideration be given as to whether criminal proceedings should be instituted.

Failure to conduct a child abuse investigation in the most effective way means the best possible protection cannot be provided for the child victim.

There must be commitment to the child and commitment to the parents/carer.

Who forms the child protection team?

This can vary between areas, but typically a team would consist of:

- 1 Detective Inspector

- 1 Detective Sergeant

- 1 Police Sergeant

- 4 Detective Constables (1 female)

- Police Constables

- 1 Office Manager (Police Constable)

- 1 Administration Officer (Civilian)

The team is CID based. It provides 24-hour cover. Officers are on call out of hours and can be reached via the switching centre. All officers have varied experience.

Terms of reference

1. To investigate, in cooperation with the local authority and other appropriate agencies, allegations and suspicions of child abuse (physical, sexual or neglect including non-organic failure to thrive and Munchausen's syndrome by proxy).

a) Occurring within the family or extended family (not stranger attacks).

b) Occurring in respect of children in care where the alleged abuser is the carer or an employee in the care organisation.

c) Where the victim is an adult person but the abuse occurred while he/she was a child under circumstances (a) or (b).

2. Where required, to assist the area major investigation pool (murder squad) in cases of murder which are the consequence of child abuse or in suspicious deaths of children (including cot deaths and deaths of children on the Child Protection Register).

3. To provide assistance and advice, in respect to interviews or liaison with the local authority and Divisional Officers investigating crimes committed against children (stranger attacks).

4. To assist the local authority and other agencies where care proceedings have been instituted and, where appropriate, to investigate such proceedings on behalf of the police.

5. To attend case conferences or strategy meetings to consider, jointly with social services and other relevant agencies, the appropriate course of action in care/control cases and to undertake agreed action.

6. To promote/partake in joint training.

7. To promote the work of the CPT inside and outside the police station.

As a rule of thumb, if a child knows who the suspected abuser is, there is a strong likelihood that the CPT will undertake the investigation.

Social Services	Health
Police	Voluntary organisations
Education system	Public
	Child protection team

Table 8.1   Agencies involved in child abuse investigation

Joint investigation

Many different agencies may share information about child abuse cases (see Table 8.1) and difficulties will be encountered in joint interagency investigations, but these can be minimised by:

- Selection of specific staff who will undergo appropriate interagency training.

- Establishing methods of joint working.

- Adopting agreed procedures for the joint interagency investigation.

This will ensure there is adequate planning and full consultation at all stages of the investigation.

Initial contact with the child (visits)

- Social services visit alone: by agreement with the police.

- Police visit alone: in an emergency.

- Visits are made jointly: this helps to minimise the trauma.

Police emergency powers

Police protection (Section 46, Children Act 1989).

- Can be any officer.

- Is there a risk of significant harm?

- Have the power to remove or prevent removal.

- Emergency Protection Order lasts 72 hours.

- Social services then have a duty to accommodate the child.

- May be a designated officer.

- They have a duty to inform the child and parents/carers.

- The child's wishes must be taken into account.

- **They have no power of entry or parental responsibility.**

When a person has not been arrested but there are grounds to suspect him of an offence, he must be cautioned before any questions are put to him. 'You do not have to say anything, but it may harm your defence if you do not mention, when questioned, something you later rely on in court. Anything you do say may be given in evidence.' Note that the police have the power of immediate entry to premises in some circumstances – by force if appropriate.

Any person may apply for an Emergency Protection Order (EPO) through application to a magistrates court.

Information must be shared with an appropriate agency if that information may influence a decision about the child.

Previous convictions involving any of the following must be recorded:

- Violence
- Child abuse
- Drugs

Conviction information can be passed on to the social services if the person concerned is about to become part of a family where there are children and the enquirer has cause for concern. In extreme cases it may be felt appropriate to disclose this information to the offender's cohabitee.

POLICE INVESTIGATION

The police investigation includes the following features:

- Statement from the child and witnesses.
- Video recording of the interview with the victim.
- Medical examination:

    forensic medical examiner

    forensic evidence

    injury evidence

- Scene exhibits:

  clothing

  bedding

  weapons

  photographic (stills/video)

Non-abusing carer/s will be involved wherever practical.

Video evidence

Following the introduction of the Criminal Justice Act, 1991, we now have a useful tool to consider using when obtaining a child's evidence (Spencer, 1991).

If the child's account of what happened is obtained in an 'evidentially sound' way, a video may be permitted to replace the child's need to give evidence-in-chief before youth/crown courts. This will be allowed if the following apply:

- The child is not the accused.

- The child is a 'competent witness'.

- The child is available for cross-examination (via closed circuit television link).

- If in violence or cruelty cases the child is under 14 at the time the video is made and under 15 at the time of the trial.

- If in sexual offences the child is under 17 at the time the video is made and under 18 at the time of the trial.

The child will be interviewed in a purpose-built video suite by a specially trained social worker and police officer complying with strict Home Office guidelines. Proper planning is essential.

Arrest/interview of suspected abusers

Suspected abusers can be detained for 24 hours, with 8 hours rest. This can be extended in exceptional circumstances (e.g. murder, rape). Within that time they must be charged or released. Interviews must be tape recorded and free legal advice may be offered.

The following outcomes are possible. The suspect may be:

- **Charged**

  in custody/on bail

  appear in magistrates or youth court.

- **Cautioned**

  admits offence

  minor nature

  recorded for 3 years.

- **Bailed to return**

  pending further enquiries

  report to Crown Prosecution Service

  report to Youth and Community Service

  Note: Police have no power to attach these conditions.

- **No follow-up**.

CROWN PROSECUTION SERVICE (CPS)

Although the police instigate proceedings, it is the responsibility of the CPS to review and, where appropriate, conduct all criminal proceedings on behalf of the police if:

- there is sufficient evidence.
- it is in the public interest.
- it is in the child's interest.
- the age and competence of the child are sufficient.
- there is a likelihood of a conviction.

The CPS may decide to prosecute which will lead to legal proceedings. They may decide to take no further action – or to offer advice or further evidence.

THE CHILD IN COURT

There is obvious trauma connected with appearing in court. However, this can be reduced by considering the following:

- Video evidence
- Pre-trial visits to the courtroom
- Use of screens
- Accompanying friend
- Witness pack (contains cut-out models of court officials to turn experience into a game).

PROBLEMS ENCOUNTERED

The child may feel guilty:

- 'It's my fault it happened.'
- 'I enjoyed it.'
- 'It's my fault the abuser was removed/family broken up.'

The child may be embarrassed in front of:

- family
- peer group
- community

This may lead to the allegation being withdrawn because:

- it may open up old wounds.
- the child cannot go through with it.
- threats may be made.

CHILD PROTECTION REGISTERS

Child Protection Registers (originally known as Non-Accidental Injury Registers) were set up throughout England and Wales in 1974 and 1975 following the recommendations of the inquiry into the death of Maria Colwell. The report emphasised the need for all agencies involved in child abuse cases to coordinate their actions. The register is kept by each social services department area.

It is not a register of all children who have been abused but of children for whom there are unresolved child protection issues and for whom there is an inter-agency child protection plan. These plans are reviewed every 6 months. Professionals concerned about a child can quickly learn of any child protection plan by making enquiries to the Child Protection Register.

Before a child is registered the case conference must decide that there is, or is a likelihood of, significant harm leading to a need for a child protection plan.

One of the following requirements needs to be satisfied:

1. There must be one or more identifiable incidents which can be described as having adversely affected the child. They may be acts of commission or omission. They can be either physical, sexual, emotional or neglectful, the specific occasion or occasions need to be identified. Professional judgement is that further incidents are likely.

2. Significant harm is expected on the basis of professional judgement of findings of the investigation in this individual case or on research evidence. The conference will need to establish so far as is possible a cause for the harm or likelihood of harm. This cause could also be applied to siblings or other children living in the same household so as to justify registration of them. Such children should be categorised according to the area of concern.

CATEGORIES OF ABUSE FOR REGISTRATION

The following categories should be used for registration. In some instances more than one category of registration may be appropriate. This should be dealt with in the child protection plan. However, multiple abuse registration should not be used to cover all eventualities.

Neglect

The persistent or severe neglect of a child, or the failure to protect a child from exposure to any kind of danger, including cold or starvation, or extreme failure to carry out important aspects of care, resulting in the significant impairment of the child's health or development, including nonorganic failure to thrive (Hobbs et al, 1993).

Physical injury

Actual or likely physical injury to a child, or failure to prevent physical injury (or suffering) to a child including deliberate poisoning, suffocation and Munchausen's syndrome by proxy (Hobbs et al, 1993). Physically injured children are categorized by the severity of their injuries:

- **Fatal:** All cases that result in death;

- **Serious:** All fractures, head injuries, internal injuries, severe burns and ingestion of toxic substances;

- **Moderate:** All soft tissue injuries of a superficial nature (Creighton and Noyes, 1989).

Sexual abuse

Actual or likely sexual exploitation of a child or adolescent. The child may be dependent and/or developmentally immature.

Emotional abuse

Actual or likely severe adverse effect on the emotional and behavioural development of a child caused by persistent or severe emotional ill-treatment or rejection. All abuse involves some emotional ill-treatment. This category should be used where it is the main or sole form of abuse (Hobbs et al, 1993).

> Placing a child's name on the register is not a magic spell which thereafter protects the child from evil. It is a way of alerting professionals to the fact that the child is thought to be at risk.
> **Liam Johnson Inquiry, 1989 (quoted by DoH, 1992)**

3 CHILD PROTECTION PROCEDURES

CHILD PRESENTING TO A and E

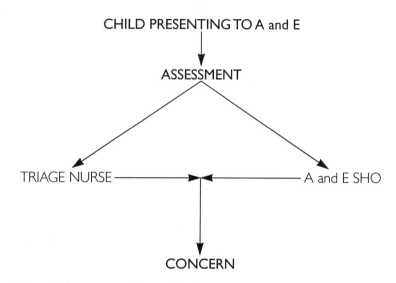

ASSESSMENT

TRIAGE NURSE ⟶ ⟵ A and E SHO

CONCERN

Possibility of abuse, unconfirmed/staff worried about a child/concern about child's circumstances/nature of attendance to A and E/relationship/interaction of parents with child/accident caused by child being neglected or in unsafe circumstances

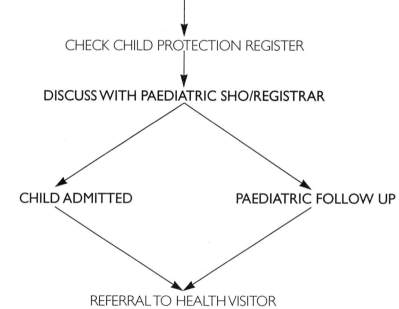

CHECK CHILD PROTECTION REGISTER

DISCUSS WITH PAEDIATRIC SHO/REGISTRAR

CHILD ADMITTED   PAEDIATRIC FOLLOW UP

REFERRAL TO HEALTH VISITOR

Figure 1

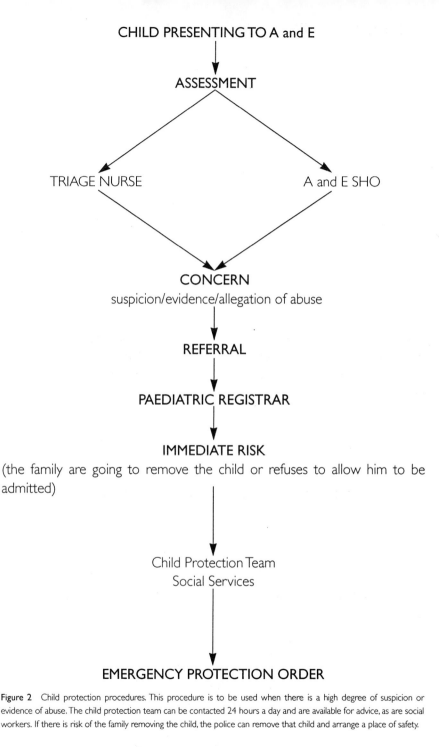

CHILD PRESENTING TO A and E

ASSESSMENT

TRIAGE NURSE   A and E SHO

CONCERN
suspicion/evidence/allegation of abuse

REFERRAL

PAEDIATRIC REGISTRAR

IMMEDIATE RISK
(the family are going to remove the child or refuses to allow him to be admitted)

Child Protection Team
Social Services

EMERGENCY PROTECTION ORDER

Figure 2 Child protection procedures. This procedure is to be used when there is a high degree of suspicion or evidence of abuse. The child protection team can be contacted 24 hours a day and are available for advice, as are social workers. If there is risk of the family removing the child, the police can remove that child and arrange a place of safety.

9

Accountability

CODE OF PROFESSIONAL CONDUCT (UKCC 1992)

All registered nurses, midwives and health visitors are personally accountable for their practice and, in the exercise of that accountability, **must**:

act always in such a manner as to promote and safeguard the interests and well-being of patients and clients.

ensure that no action or omission on your part, or within your sphere of responsibility, is detrimental to the interests, condition or safety of patients and clients.
UKCC 1992

RESPONSIBILITIES

Personal

- Recognise that you need to update your knowledge and be aware of current research.

- Be able to recognise signs of child abuse.

- Acknowledge that child abuse exists.

- Trying to safeguard family values.

- Be aware that child abuse exists in a cycle form and recognise that you are trying to break the cycle and not break up the family.

- You are professionally responsible under your code of conduct to safeguard patients.

- Work as part of a team and recognise everybody's role.

- Ensure good communication between disciplines – pass on fears and suspicions to ensure children do not slip through the net.

- Be aware of responsibilities to update and educate other members of staff in the management of child abuse.

- Be the child's advocate.

THE NURSE'S ROLE

- Be aware and follow triage guidelines.

- Be aware of signs of child abuse.

- Make careful documentation of:

  what the child tells you

  what parents say

  physical findings.

- Pass on concerns to relevant staff.

- Be aware of policies and procedures in the management of child abuse.

- Consult other agencies involved in the management of child abuse for help and advice.

- Be an effective, confident and proficient member of the team involved in caring for children.

References

Asher R (1951) Cited in Meadow R (1993) *ABC of Child Abuse*, 2nd edn. London: British Medical Association.

Bamford F and **Roberts R** (1993) Child Sexual Abuse. In: Meadow R (ed.) *ABC of Child Abuse*. London: British Medical Association.

Browne K, Davies C and **Stratton P** (1991) *Early Prediction and Prevention of Child Abuse*. Chichester: Wiley.

Butler–Sloss E (1988) *Report of the Enquiry into Child Abuse in Cleveland 1987*. London: HMSO.

Caffey J (1946) Cited in Hobbs CJ, Hanks HG and Wynne JM (1993) *Child Abuse and Neglect*. London: Churchill Livingstone.

Cantwell H and **Rosenberg D** (1993) The Consequences of Neglect – Individual and Societal. In: Hobbs CJ and Wynne JM (1993) *Clinical Paediatrics*. London: Baillière Tindall.

Creighton SJ (1984) *Trends in Child Abuse*. London: NSPCC.

Creighton SJ and **Noyes P** (1989) *Child Abuse Trends in England and Wales, 1983–87*. London: NSPCC.

Creighton SJ and **Noyes P** (1990) *Child Abuse in 1989: Research Briefing Paper 11*. London: NSPCC.

Crouse KA (1992) Munchausen syndrome by proxy: recognising the victim. *Paediatric Nursing*, **18**(3): 249–252.

De Mause L (1980) Cited in Hobbs CJ, Hanks HG and Wynne JM (1993) *Child Abuse and Neglect*. London: Churchill Livingstone.

Department of Health (1989) *The Children Act – An Introductory Guide for the NHS*. London: DoH, HMSO.

Department of Health (1992) *Children and Young Persons on Child Protection Register, Year Ending 31 March 1991, England*. HMSO: London.

Egeland B (1991) Cited in Browne K, Davies C and Stratton P (1991) *Early Prediction and Prevention of Child Abuse*. London: Wiley.

Feldman KW and **Brewer DF** (1984) Child abuse, cardiopulmonary resuscitation and rib fractures. *Paediatrics* **73**: 339–342.

Fischoff J (1975) Cited in Hobbs CJ and Wynne JM (1993) *Clinical Paediatrics*. London: Baillière Tindall.

Francis J (1993) Positive protection. *Community Care*, April, 18–19.

Frothingham TE (1991) Cited in Hobbs CJ, Hanks HG and Wynne JM (1993) *Child Abuse and Neglect*. London: Churchill Livingstone.

Garbarino J, Guthman E and **Seeley JW** (1988) *The Psychologically Battered Child*. San Francisco: Jossey Bass.

Garbarino J (1992) *Emotional Abuse – Practice Paper*, 1st edn, 10–11.

Gellert BGA (1989) Cited in Hobbs CJ, Hanks HG and Wynne JM (1993) *Child Abuse and Neglect*. London: Churchill Livingstone.

Gillespie FJ (1993) Child sexual abuse 1: definitions, incidence and consequences. *British Journal of Nursing* **2**(5): 267–272.

Goodwin JM (1989) Cited in Hobbs CJ, Hanks HG and Wynne JM (1993) *Child Abuse and Neglect*. London: Churchill Livingstone.

Hanks HG et al (1988) Cited in Hobbs CJ, Hanks HG and Wynne JM (1993) *Child Abuse and Neglect*. London: Churchill Livingstone.

Helfer RE (1990) The neglect of our children. *Paediatric Clinics of North America* **37**: 4.

Herndon WA (1983) Cited in Hobbs CJ (1993) Fractures. In: Meadow R (ed.) *ABC of Child Abuse*. London. British Medical Association.

Hobbs CJ (1991) Cited in Hobbs CJ, Hanks HG and Wynne JM (1993) *Child Abuse and Neglect*. London: Churchill Livingstone.

Hobbs CJ (1993a) Fractures. In: Meadow R (ed.) *ABC of Child Abuse*. London. British Medical Association.

Hobbs CJ (1993b) Head Injuries. In: Meadow R (ed.) *ABC of Child Abuse.* London. British Medical Association.

Hobbs CJ (1993c) Burns and Scalds. In: Meadow R (ed.) *ABC of Child Abuse.* London. British Medical Association.

Hobbs CJ, Hanks HG and **Wynne JM** (1993) *Child Abuse and Neglect.* London: Churchill Livingstone.

Hobbs CJ and **Wynne JM** (1990) The sexually abused battered child. *Archives of Disease in Childhood* **65**: 423–427.

Hobbs CJ and **Wynne JM** (1993) *Clinical Paediatrics.* London: Baillière Tindall.

Illingworth RS (1983) Cited in Hobbs CJ and Wynne JM (1993) *Clinical Paediatrics.* London: Baillière Tindall.

Jobling M (1976) *The Abused Child.* London: National Children's Bureau.

Johnson CF (1990) Cited in Hobbs CJ, Hanks HG and Wynne JM (1993) *Child Abuse and Neglect.* London: Churchill Livingstone.

Jurgrau A (1990) How to spot child abuse. *RN*, October, 26–33.

Kempe RS and **Kempe CH** (1978) *Child Abuse.* Glasgow: Fontana.

Kempe RS et al (1962) Cited in Hobbs CJ, Hanks HG and Wynne JM (1993) *Child Abuse and Neglect.* London: Churchill Livingstone.

Kitzinger J (1990) Cited in Saines J (1992) A considered response to an emotional crisis. *Professional Nurse* **8**(3): 148–152.

Leatherland J (1986) Do you know child abuse when you see it? *RN*, November, 28–30.

Meadow R (ed.) (1993) *ABC of Child Abuse*, 2nd edn. London. British Medical Association.

Newson J and **Newson E** (1986) Cited in Hobbs CJ, Hanks HG and Wynne JM (1993) *Child Abuse and Neglect.* London: Churchill Livingstone.

NSPCC (1984) Cited in Creighton SJ (1984) Trends in Child Abuse. London: NSPCC.

NSPCC (1990) Cited in Hobbs CJ, Hanks HG and Wynne JM (1993) *Child Abuse and Neglect.* London: Churchill Livingstone.

Robinson R (1991) Physical signs of sexual abuse in children. *British Medical Journal* **302**: 863–864.

Rosenberg DA (1987) Cited in Hobbs CJ, Hanks HG and Wynne JM (1993) *Child Abuse and Neglect*. London: Churchill Livingstone.

Russell DEH (1986) Cited in Hobbs CJ, Hanks HG and Wynne JM (1993) *Child Abuse and Neglect*. London: Churchill Livingstone.

Scherb BJ (1988) Suspected abuse and neglect of children. *Journal of Emergency Nursing* **14**(1): 44–47.

Lord Shaftesbury (1880) Cited in: Meadow R (ed.) *ABC of Child Abuse*. London. British Medical Association.

Skuse D (1993) Emotional abuse and neglect. In: Meadow R (ed.) *ABC of Child Abuse*. London: British Medical Journal.

Smith SM and **Hanson R** (1974) Cited in Hobbs CJ, Hanks HG and Wynne JM (1993) *Child Abuse and Neglect*. London: Churchill Livingstone.

Speight N (1993) Non-accidental injury. In: Meadow R (ed.) *ABC of Child Abuse*. London. British Medical Association.

Spencer, J (1991) Cited in Hobbs CJ, Hanks HG and Wynne JM (1993) *Child Abuse and Neglect*. London: Churchill Livingstone.

Spitz RA (1948) Cited in Hobbs CJ, Hanks HG and Wynne JM (1993) *Child Abuse and Neglect*. London: Churchill Livingstone.

Summit R (1983) The child sexual abuse accommodation syndrome. *Child Abuse and Neglect*. **7**: 177–193.

United Kingdom Central Council for Nursing, Midwifery and Health Visiting (1992) *Code of Professional Conduct*, 3rd edn. London: UKCC.

Wisslow SL (1990) Cited in Hobbs CJ, Hanks HG and Wynne JM (1993) *Child Abuse and Neglect*. London: Churchill Livingstone.

Wolf S (1988) Cited in Hobbs CJ, Hanks HG and Wynne JM (1993) *Child Abuse and Neglect*. London: Churchill Livingstone.

Worlock P et al (1986) Cited in Hobbs CJ, Hanks HG and Wynne JM (1993) *Child Abuse and Neglect*. London: Churchill Livingstone.

Wynne JM (1988) Cited in Hobbs CJ, Hanks HG and Wynne JM (1993) *Child Abuse and Neglect*. London: Churchill Livingstone.

Bibliography

Barker W (1990) The aetiology of child sexual abuse. *Community Outlook*, April, 25–26.

Buchanan MFG (1985) The recognition of non-accidental injury in children. *The Practitioner* **229**: 815–819.

Crow J (1993) Safety net. *Nursing Times* **89**(10): 42–44.

De Jongh J (1988) Do you know when a child's at risk? *Australian Nurses' Journal* **18**(4): 14–15.

Dingwall R (1987) Now tick the scapegoat of your choice. *Nursing Times* **83**(40): 33–35.

Dundon M and **Bates A** (1993) Raising public awareness of child abuse issues. *Health Visitor* **66**(1): 22–23.

Dunn M (1989) Realities of Cleveland. *Nursing Times* **85**(10): 28–31.

Fawcett-Hensey A (1985) Jasmine: the lessons to be learned. *Nursing Times* **81**: 18–19.

Fumpson J and **Stout P** (1985) Suffer little children. ... *Nursing Times* **81**: 38–39.

Greenland C (1986) Preventing child abuse and neglect deaths: The identification and management of high risk cases. *Health Visitor* **59**: 205–206.

Hempel S (1993) Child abuse. *Community Outlook*, January, 25–27.

Heywood Jones I (1988) Home is where the hurt is. *Nursing Times* **346**: 48–49.

Johnston C (1988) Last chance for change? *Nursing Times* **84**(7): 30–31.

Kowalczuk LS (1990) Triage decisions: A 24-month-old infant with painful urination. *Journal of Emergency Nursing* **16**(2): 124–125.

Ladjali M (1993) Female genital mutilation. *British Medical Journal* **307**: 460.

Lask B (1992) Talking with children. *British Journal of Hospital Medicine* **47**(9): 688–690.

Laurance J (1988) Blaming the messenger. *New Statesman and Society*, July, 13–15.

Laurance J (1988) Statistics of taboo. *New Statesman and Society*, July, 33–34.

Laurant C (1991) Spotting trouble in A&E. *Nursing Times* **87**(19): 56–57.

Moore J (1985) For the children's sake. *Nursing Times* **161**: 19–20.

Murphy G (1990) Physical and sexual abuse. *Paediatric Nursing*, May, 22–23.

Neasham J (1989) Suffering little children. *Nursing Times* **85**(24): 64.

O'Brien C (1992) Medical and forensic examination by a sexual assault nurse examiner of a 7-year-old victim of sexual assault. *Journal of Emergency Nursing* **18**(3): 199–204.

Patel F (1992) Artefact in forensic medicine: Childhood iatrogenic oral injury. *Police Surgeon* **41**: 8–9.

Pithers D (1989) A guide through the maze of child protection. *Social Work Today*, January, 18–19.

Qureshi B (1988) Cultural aspects of child abuse in Britain. *Midwife, Health Visitor and Community Nurse* **24**(10): 412–413.

Sadler C (1986) News focus. *Nursing Times* **82**: 16–17.

Skuse DH (1987) Child sex abuse in general practice: recognition and response. *Practitioner* **231**: 706–711.

Sluckin A (1989) Looking out for emotional abuse. *Midwife, Health Visitor and Community Nurse* **25**(3): 93–96.

Stainton Rogers W (1989) Child abuse and neglect. *Community Outlook*, March, 21–22.

Torkington S (1989) Accountability and training in child protection work. *Senior Nurse* **9**(1): 10–11.

Turner T (1988) After Cleveland. *Nursing Times,* **84**(28): 18.

Valman HB (1987) Child abuse. *British Medical Journal* **294:** 633–635.

Visentin L (1988) Child abuse. *Nursing Standard* **2:** 29.

Index

Note: numbers in **bold** indicate where the main discussion occurs, numbers in *italic* indicate where a table appears

Abdominal injuries 7
  bruising in sexual abuse 41
Abduction, child 26
Accident and Emergency (A&E) 7–8
  assessment in 8–9
  child behaviour in 9
  child protection procedures 78–9
  incidence of child abuse seen in 7
Accident-prone child 6
Accommodation syndrome 27–8
  delayed disclosure 28
  entrapment and accommodation 28
  helplessness 27–8
  retraction 28
  secrecy 27
Accountability 81–2
Alcohol
  physical abuse and 9
  sexual abuse and 26
Alopecia, traumatic 19
Anal intercourse *see* Buggery
Anal tags 38
Anxiety
  as effect of sexual abuse 30
  parental 6

Battered baby syndrome 15
Bed-wetting *see* Toileting
  misdemeanours
Belts, bruising from 14
Bereavement 5

Bite marks
  bruising from 15
  sexual abuse 42
Black eye 14
Bruises 4, 13–15
  age by appearance 13
  bite marks 15
  bizarre marks 15
  fractures 15–18
  hand marks 14
  kicks 15
  made by implements 14
  patterns 14–15
  in sexual abuse 13
Buggery 29, 36
  anal dilatation 39
  external trauma 38
  signs of 38–9
Burns 20–3
  accidental 22
  assessment *23*
  delay in seeking help 5
  incidence 21
  in sexual abuse 41, 42
  sites of 22
  types 21–2
Buttocks, burns, in sexual abuse 22, 30

Candidiasis 40
Carers *see* Parents/care-givers
Cerebral contusion 19

Cerebral oedema 19
Chemical burns 22
Child's right of refusal 67
Child Assessment Order 67
Child Protection Registers 12, 76
  categories of abuse for 76–7
Child Protection Team 68–72
  composition 69
  contact with child 71
  joint investigation 71
  police emergency powers 71
  police focus 69
  role of 68
  terms of reference 69–70
Children Act (1989)
  Child Assessment Order 67
  child protection aspects 66
  child's right of refusal 67
  emergency protection orders 67
  main principles 65–6
  medical examination and assessment of
    children 67
Choking, bruises indicating 14
Cigarette burns 4, 21, 22
Code of Professional Conduct 81
Colwell, Maria 76
Constipation 39, 40
Cot death see Sudden infant death syndrome
Court, child appearance in 75
Criminal Justice Act (1991) 73
Crohn's disease 39, 40
Crown Prosecution Service 74–5

Death see Fatal abuse; Sudden infant death
  syndrome
Depression as effect of sexual abuse 30
Developmental delay 47
Drug abuse 9, 41

Ears, bruises to 13
Eczema, atopic 40
Electrical burns 21
Emergency Protection Orders 67, 71
Emotional abuse 43–5
  amongst physically abused children 12
  categories 44

as category of abuse for registration 77
  definition 43
  identification 44–5
  incidence 43
  manifestation 45
  in Munchausen's syndrome by proxy 57
Emotional neglect 47
Exhibitionism 30
Extrafamilial abuse 26

Face
  bruises 19
  burns on 22
  fracture 19
Failure to thrive 4, **52–4**, 77
  case studies 54
  definitions 52–3
  non-organic 47, 52
  organic 52
  parents' behaviour 53
Family size 12
Fatal abuse **61–4**
  age of child and 61
  incidence 12, 61
  poisoning 63–4
  presentation 62
Feet, burns on 22
'Flashing' 30
Forced feeding 14
Fractures 4, 15–18
  abuse or accident 15–16
  delay in seeking help 5
  metaphyseal and periphyseal 17
  pattern of injury in abuse 17
  rib 17
  of shafts of long bones 18
  significance of *16*
Friction burns 22
Frozen watchfulness 45

Gags, bruising from 14
Genitalia
  bruising of 13
  burning, in sexual abuse 30
  examination of 36–8
Gonorrhoea 42

Handicapped children, physical abuse of 12
Hands, burns on 22
Head injuries 4, 7, 18–20
    categories 19
    site and extent *19*
History of child abuse 1
History, features of 5–6
    discrepant history 5
    family crisis 5
    history-taking from care giver 8
    history-taking from child 8
    parental history of abuse 5
    social isolation 6
    trigger factors 5
    unrealistic expectations 6
    unreasonable delay 5
HIV infection 41

Incidence of child abuse 1
Infanticide *see* Fatal abuse
Institutional abuse 26
Intracrural intercourse 30, 38
Intrafamilial abuse 26

Kicks, bruising from 15

Ligatures, bruising from 14
Love-bites 41
Lying 5

Management of child abuse **65–79**
Masturbation 29, 36
Medical examination and assessment of
    children 67
Metaphyseal fractures 17
Mouth, burns around 22
Multidisciplinary teamwork 41
Munchausen's syndrome by proxy 11,
    55–60, 77
    consequences 57
    definition 55–6
    doctor shopping 56
    enforced invalidism 56–7
    fabricated illness 57, *58*

    features of abuser 59–60
    management 60
    perceived illness 56
    poisoning in 64
    sudden infant death syndrome and 63
    warning signs 57–9

Neglect 4, **46–51**
    case studies 50–1
    as category of abuse for registration 77
    death from 62
    definition 46
    incidence 46
    indications 47
    physical manifestations/consequences *48*
    social status 47
Non-Accidental Injury Registers *see* Child
    Protection Registers
Nurse's role 82

Oral sex 29, 36

Paedophilic sexual orientation 27
Parent–infant stress syndrome 15
Parents/care-givers
    anger in 9
    anxiety 6
    attitude and behaviour 9
    behaviour of 5
    defensive behaviour 9
    failure to thrive and behaviour of 53
    history of abuse 5, 26
    see also Munchausen's syndrome by
        proxy
Perineal bruising 38
Periphyseal fractures 17
Petechiae
    in cot death syndrome 63
    as sign of sexual abuse 40
Physical abuse **11–23**
    age 12
    bruises 13–15
    burns and scalds 20–1
    combined with sexual abuse 40–1
    definition 11

Physical abuse (*continued*)
fractures 15–18
gender differences in 12
head injuries in 18–20
incidence 12
reporting of 11
retinal haemorrhage 20
skeletal survey 18
social background 12
Physical injury
as category of abuse for registration 77
Poisoning
accidental 63
deliberate 62, 64, 77
presentation 64
Police and Criminal Evidence (PACE) Act
(1984) 72
Police investigation 72–4
arrest/interview of suspected abusers
73–4
video evidence 73
Pornography 30
Poverty 12
Pregnancy 42
Presentation 4
direct report 4
incidental discovery of an injury 4
of an injury 4
Prostitution 30, 41

Radiant burns 22
Rape 29, 31
Rectal tumour 40
Reflex anal dilatation 36, 39
Relationships, difficulty with, as effect of
sexual abuse 30
Rent boys 30
Responsibilities
personal 81
professional 82
Retinal haemorrhage 3, 15, 20
Rib fractures 4, 17

Scalds 20, 21
in sexual abuse 41
Scalp, bruises 19

Self-injury 30
Sex rings 26, 27
Sexual abuse 4, **25–42**
accommodation syndrome 27–8
age of child 32
bruising in 13, 14
burns in 21
as category of abuse for registration 78
characteristics of abusers 27–8
combined with physical abuse 12, 40–1
contact 28–9
definition 25
degrees of force and violence 31–2
differential diagnosis 40
disclosure 33, 35–6, 42
essential characteristics 27
examination of genitalia 36–8
factors affecting outcome in child 31–3
frequency and duration 31
gender 25
HIV infection 41
incidence 25
intercrural intercourse 38
long-term effects on adults 30–1
long-term effects on child, adapted to
Maslow's human needs 33–5
multiple abusers 33
non-contact 29
patterns of 26
physical evidence 36
relationship with offender 32
risk factors 26–7
role of medical staff 36, 37
short-term effects on child 30
signs associated with 39–40
signs of buggery 38–9
types 28–9, 31
Shaftesbury, Lord 1
Shaken baby syndrome 20
Skeletal survey 18
Skull fractures 19
Social background
in physical abuse 12
Spina bifida 40
Stealing 5
Straps, bruising from 14
Street abuse 26
Streptococcal cellulitis 40

Subarachnoid haemorrhage 19
Subdural haematoma 4, 15
Subdural haemorrhage 19, 20
Subgaleal haematoma 19
Sudden infant death syndrome (cot death)
    62–3
    clinical features 62
    incidence 62
    Munchausen syndrome by proxy and
        63
    suffocation 62
    warning features 63
Suffocation 11, 77
Supervision neglect 47

Ties, bruising from 14
Toileting misdemeanours
    bruising in 13
    burns as punishment for 22
    as effect of sexual abuse 30
    as trigger for physical abuse 5

Unemployment 12

Vaginal intercourse 29, 36

Warts, genital 39
Withdrawal as effect of sexual abuse 30